HALEY'S HANDY HINTS

1001
PRACTICAL IDEAS!

by Gale McDougall
and
Graham & Rosemary Haley

Second Printing 1989
Third Printing 1991

Thanks are extended to the many homemakers from coast to coast who contributed tips and ideas on homemaking for both our T.V. series and this publication. We're grateful you have shared your knowledge with us.

Published in Canada by
3H Productions Inc.
P.O. Box 114, Station "Z",
Toronto, Ontario, Canada
M5N 2Z3

I.S.B.N. 0-9692873-0-5

CONTENTS

NOTES:

HINTS BY THE BAKER'S DOZEN!

Oops! I've Run Out Of:

Baking Powder ... Use 1 tsp. tartar plus ½ tsp. baking soda to replace 2 tblsp. baking powder.

Sugar ... Use 1 cup honey plus ¼ tsp. baking soda to replace 1 cup of white sugar. Remember to deduct 3 tblsp. liquid from the recipe.

  ° Or use 1 ¼ cups of fruit sugar or brown sugar to substitute for 1 cup of white sugar.

Eggs ... If the recipe calls for more than two eggs, one egg can be omitted but add 2 tblsp. milk and ½ tsp. baking powder to replace it.

Chocolate ... Replace 1 square of chocolate with 3 tblsp. cocoa and 1 tsp. shortening.

Cornstarch ... Flour can be substituted for cornstarch if you double the quantity.

Also See Emergency Substitutions p. 120

Cakes, Pies & Frostings

  ° Before cutting fresh, moist cake, run a thin bladed knife under hot water and dry. Slices without crumbling.

  ° After the cake has been cut, keep it moist by slicing fresh bread to the size of the exposed cake. Secure with toothpicks.

  ° Cake won't stick to the pan if you grease beforehand with unsalted fat and dust with flour.

  ° Another stick-free method is to thoroughly grease a piece of clean brown paper that has been cut to fit the cake pan. Foolproof!

  ° Dip plastic cookie cutters in warm salad oil to prevent dough from sticking.

  ° Baked apples won't crack if you peel a ½" band around the middle of the apple prior to baking.

  ° Try rolling some grated cheese into pastry dough when making apple pie.

- Eliminate soggy crusts when baking fruit pies by brushing the bottom crust with egg white before adding fruit. This helps prevent the juice from soaking through.

- To keep fruit cakes moist while baking, place a pan of water along side of it in the oven and keep replacing the water until cake is done.

- Prevent meringue from sticking to the knife by adding a pinch of cream of tartar to egg whites when beating them.

- Place a layer of chocolate mint patties over a baked cake and return it to the oven until the patties have softened. Spread with a spatula for a delicious icing.

- Or, sprinkle cinnamon and sugar right on top of the cake batter for an "instant" sweet topping.

- A pinch of salt and a tablespoon of cornstarch for every two cups of icing sugar will help take away that "too sweet" taste.

- Use vegetable oil to lubricate egg beaters for an easy cleanup.

- Or, lubricate with glycerin before using.

- Just a pinch of salt added to egg whites makes beating a quick and easy job.

- Before frosting cake, cut triangles of waxed paper to cover cake dish. Let several inches overlap. Place pointed end of triangle in centre of dish. Place unfrosted cake on top. When frosting is completed, slide each piece of waxed paper out slowly. You will have a sparkling clean cake dish.

- Fudge frosting will stay soft and workable if you place the bowl in a pan of hot water.

- No cake decorating utensil? Cut the end off an empty quart milk bag and wash it out. Clip a small opening at the opposite end. Fill the bag with frosting and squeeze through small hole to decorate!

- Shredded coconut that has dried out is delicious toasted and sprinkled over desserts. Sprinkle on a cookie sheet and bake in a medium oven, shaking occasionally.

- Before using raisins in baking, let them sit in warm water for a few minutes to make them plump and juicy.

○ If your recipe calls for miniature marshmallows and you have on hand the larger variety, simply cut with scissors dusted with flour.

○ For the flakiest upper crust on pies, brush lightly with cold water just before popping in the oven. Melts in your mouth!

Measuring The Easy Way ... Honey, syrup or other sticky liquids will slide out of the measuring cup with ease if the cup is oiled lightly before use.

○ Pour cold water into your measuring cup. If you need ½ cup of shortening, fill half the cup with water and then put your shortening in until it reaches the full cup mark. Also works well with butter, hard margarine.

Softening Brown Sugar ... A slice of fresh bread placed with the hardened brown sugar in a plastic bag and sealed tightly will soften the sugar in about three hours.

○ If you really need brown sugar in a hurry, try running it through a hand grater.

○ Or, put hard brown sugar in an oven-proof bowl. Alongside place another bowl filled with water. Set in a low heat oven for an hour.

Breads, Rolls, Crackers

Heating Bread Or Rolls ... Use large foil potato chip bags to heat rolls and bread in the oven. Saves $$$.

Loafing Around ... Bread you slice yourself stays fresher longer.

○ Day-old bread makes better toast than fresh bread.

Crispy Crackers ... Keep soda crackers in the bottom drawer of the stove. The heat from the oven will keep them crisp.

○ Crackers, pretzels and potato chips that have lost their crunch can be revived by placing on a cookie sheet and broiling for just a minute.

Next Day Muffins ... Revive stale muffins. Sprinkle with drops of water, place in a paper bag and warm in a hot oven for 5 to 10 minutes.

A Few "Crumby" Ideas ... Cut stale bread into ½ inch cubes. Place on a baking sheet and bake at 325°F for 15 minutes, stirring occasionally. If desired sprinkle with seasonings such as garlic or celery salt before baking. Lovely salad croutons.

- Dry bread in an oven at 300°F for 10 minutes. Break into pieces and place in a paper bag. Secure end and crush with a rolling pin to make bread crumbs.

- Toss stale bread cubes and crusts in a blender to make bread crumbs.

Dairy Products

Butter Extender... Stretch a pound of butter into two by following these steps: Bring butter to room temperature and beat to cream with a mixer. Slowly add 2 cups of evaporated milk and continue beating until mixture is smooth. Chill to a solid.

Cheese ... Cheese that has dried out can still be used. Simply grate and store for use with soups or vegetables.

- Make a delicious spread with dried out cheese by blending with raw onions and your favorite seasonings.

Eggs, Eggs, Eggs ... Eggs should be stored with the large end up. This keeps the air pocket in the large end and the yolk in the centre.

- Always keep eggs refrigerated and remove ½ hour before cooking, for best results.

- Eggs won't crack if you make a small hole with a needle in the large end of the egg before boiling.

- No egg poacher? Use the rims from preserve jars and lightly grease the inside of the rim to prevent eggs from sticking. Place required number of rims into the pan and break eggs into them. Add a drop of lemon juice to the water when poaching to keep egg whites from spreading.

- Or, use regular metal jar lids, grease and place upside down in the pan.

- When slicing hard boiled eggs, dip your knife in water periodically to prevent yolks from crumbling.

- When a piece of egg shell falls into the bowl, remove it by using the large broken half of the egg shell. The small piece will cling to the larger shell for easy removal.

- When beating eggs separately, beat the whites first. They won't cling to the beater the way yolks will, saving you a wash up.

- When you only need the white of an egg and not the yolk, economize by cutting ¼" square in one end of the shell and allowing the white to drop through. Seal the hole with a small piece of tape and cover the entire shell with foil. You'll have a fresh yolk when you need it.

- The freshness of eggs can be determined by these simple methods. Fresh eggs will sink in water; shells are rough and dull (if it's smooth and shiny, don't use it); contents should feel firm, not loose, when shaken lightly.

- Eggs are more easily separated when cold.

- A small kitchen funnel is a handy tool when separating yolks and whites. The yolks will remain in the funnel.

- Egg yolks can be kept fresh for several days by covering with cold water and refrigerating.

- The texture of eggs will be tough if you salt them during the frying process.

- Boiled eggs should never be boiled! Simmering to doneness will produce tastier results.

- To prevent boiled eggs from cracking, let stand in warm water for a few minutes prior to cooking.

- Save energy! Boil eggs in the bottom half of a double boiler while cooking cereal in the top half.

Milk That Has Taken A Turn ... Don't pour out sour milk — it can still go a long way. If it's just beginning to turn, a pinch of baking soda can restore freshness. But if it's really sour, you can still use it in gravies and for baking by adding 2 tsp. baking soda for each cup of milk. (Reduce baking powder in your recipe by 2 tsp.)

But On The Other Hand ... If your recipe calls for sour milk and you don't have any, add 2 tblsp. of vinegar to 1 cup of sweet milk and stir.

No More Scorching ... A pan rinsed in cold water before using to heat milk will prevent milk from sticking.

- Adding a pinch of salt to scorched milk removes the 'burnt' taste.

How To Whip Whipping Cream ... Make sure cream and all utensils are cooled before starting. Keep the bowl in a pan of ice cold water throughout the whipping process. Add a drop or two of lemon juice if the cream is still not stiffening.

'Fruity' Tips

Non-Browning Apples... When peeling a quantity of apples, place peeled apples in a basin of cold, slightly salted water to prevent browning.

- When making a fresh fruit salad, keep cut fruit from browning by placing it in a bowl of grapefruit juice.

Don't Toss Out That Banana... Save it for making banana breads and cakes. Mash the darkened bananas with a potato masher and freeze in a plastic container.

Removing Fruit Stains From Hands... To remove strawberry or other fruit stains from your hands, rub with a paste of cornmeal and lemon juice.

Did You Know... Honeydew is the only melon that continues to sweeten after it has been cut from the vine.

Lemon-Aids... Get almost twice the juice from a lemon by heating it first. Place lemon in a saucepan of water, bring to a boil, remove to cool, slice and squeeze.

- Before cutting lemons, roll gently on the cutting board using a little hand pressure as you roll. You'll be surprised at how much more juice is extracted.

When Making Orange Juice... You will get more juice from an orange if it is allowed to warm to room temperature first. To achieve the same effect quickly, hold oranges under hot running water for a few minutes.

- Save orange & lemon rinds. Grate, place in a plastic bag and keep in the freezer for use in drinks, breads, cakes, etc.

The Produce Counter

Remember... Soaking fresh vegetables in water for too long a period reduces vitamin content. Similarly, using soda when cooking green vegetables may create an appetizing appearance, but most of the important nutrients will be decreased.

Is That Cabbage I Smell?... Placing a heel of bread on top of cauliflower, broccoli, cabbage or brussel sprouts while cooking will help to eliminate cooking odors.

- A spoonful of sugar added to boiling turnip prevents odors.

- A whole walnut added to boiling cabbage will eliminate odor.

○ Or, add a stalk or two of celery to the boiling cabbage water.

Maintain Maximum Nutritional Value! ... For long vegetables such as carrots slice lengthwise to retain nutrients.

Sweet Corn ... A teaspoon of lemon juice added to boiling sweet corn on the cob will keep the corn a bright yellow color.

Cute Cukes ... Make an attractive scalloped edge on thinly sliced cucumbers by running the tines of a fork lengthwise over the cucumber before slicing.

Turning Green Tomatoes Red ... Keep green tomatoes firm through the ripening process by storing stem-up in a shady place.

○ Or place them in a damp cloth and store in a paper bag.

Flavor Adders ... Celery tops and pea pods are terrific flavor-adders in soups and stews.

No Tear Onions ... Ever wondered why onions make you cry? A certain liquid ingredient present in onions evaporates when the onion has been cut and the liquid is exposed to the air. The liquid film in our eyes is especially sensitive to this evaporated substance, and we produce tears to wash it away! Eliminate the problem of tears by refrigerating the onion for an hour before cutting. (The cold substance evaporates more slowly.) Or run the onion under cold water as you slice it.

Potatoes And Nutrition ... Instead of peeling potatoes, scour with a metal sponge and rinse well. It's quick, easy and saves valuable nutrients close to the skin.

○ Pour boiling water over potatoes just before peeling to allow you to peel thinly and easily.

Instant Baked Potatoes! ... Boil potatoes whole for 15 minutes before placing in a hot oven. Saves half the baking time.

Creamy Mashed Potatoes ... Mashed potatoes will be light and fluffy if milk is heated and added before mashing.

○ Add brown sugar and butter to mashed sweet potatoes and stuff in empty orange shells. Brown in the oven for a few minutes and watch those eyes light up!

Home Fries ... Sprinkle potatoes to be fried with flour. They'll be deliciously golden brown. Try adding a little paprika and garlic salt for extra taste.

Sweet Peas . . . Instead of adding sugar to sweeten fresh peas during cooking, try adding several empty pea pods to the pot. Economical and tasty!

White & Bright . . . Cauliflower will be snowy white if soaked in cold salted water for ½ hour prior to cooking.

Rice That Won't Stick . . . Add a spoonful of lemon juice to boiling rice to keep grains from sticking together.

Tastier Rice . . . Add fruit or vegetable juice instead of water to rice for a great taste!

Pasta . . . A few drops of oil added to boiling water when cooking pasta will prevent spillovers onto the stove and will also keep the pasta from sticking to the pot.

Ugly But Cheap Tomatoes . . . Save money by deliberately buying misshapen or scarred tomatoes. The taste is not affected.

Crisping Wilted Vegetables . . . Add a few drops of lemon juice or cider vinegar to a bowl of ice cold water. Add wilted lettuce and let stand for an hour.

- Wash and wrap vegetables in paper towels before placing in the refrigerator.

- Add a few slices of raw potato to a pan of cold water and allow celery stalks and lettuce leaves to crisp for ½ hour.

- Stand stems of wilted asparagus in cold water for a while and watch them come back to life.

- Don't throw away unattractive wilted lettuce leaves. Crisp them in cold water and shred for use in sandwiches or salads.

- Coat green peppers with olive oil before stuffing and baking to maintain their original color.

Meats, Fish & Gravies

Hamburger Stretchers . . . Crushed cereals or bread crumbs added to hamburger will make it go a little farther.

Fast Hamburgers . . . Poke a hole in the centre of the burger before frying. This helps to cook the centre as quickly as the outside.

Gravy Too Thin? . . . Slowly add a mixture of cornstarch or flour and water to gravy, bringing to a slow boil. Stir constantly. For nutritious and great tasting gravy, remember to use water in which vegetables have been cooked or canned.

Gravy Too Thick? ... Add water or vegetable "juices".

Making Gravy ... Creamy smooth gravy can be made by substituting half the usual amount of flour with cornstarch.

- If the gravy turns out to be too greasy, try adding a pinch of baking soda. Sprinkle roast pan with flour and brown well before adding liquid.

- When roasting meat, place a small pan of flour beside the roast pan in the oven. The flour will brown nicely for use when making gravy.

To The Rescue ... Add raw potatoes to reduce saltiness in stews or soups. Remove potatoes when cooked. Or add sugar.

- Add a tsp. of cider vinegar and 1 tsp. of sugar to reduce saltiness.

- If your stew or soup recipe turns out to be too sweet, try adding a little salt or a spoonful of cider vinegar.

- To remove excess fat from soup, toss in a lettuce leaf. It will absorb the fat and can be thrown away.

Fish ... place filets of fish on lettuce leaves when baking to prevent sticking to the pan. Discard leaves when fish is baked.

- When handling fish, moisten fingertips with water and dip them in salt. This helps prevent fish from sliding out of your grip and cuts down on the odor left on hands.

Clams & Oysters ... Hard shell clams can be easily opened by pouring boiling water over them first.

- Try rolling oysters in cracker crumbs seasoned with celery salt before frying. Delicious!

Reduce Sausage Shrinkage ... and remove excess fats. Boil sausages for 5 to 10 minutes and roll in flour before frying or broiling.

Bacon ... Bacon drippings are an economical and delicious seasoning. Keep drippings in good condition by following these steps. Use small jars for storage so bottom layers are used before spoiling. Date jars as you use them, using oldest jar first.

- Remove sediment from fat by frying raw potato slices until brown. Potatoes will absorb most sediment while soaking up any extraneous flavors.

- If your bacon curls up when you're frying it, try dipping the pieces in cold water first.

Remember... when substituting bacon fat for shortening, always reduce quantity by 25% to achieve same effect.

Catchy Kitchen Hints

Stickless Frying ... Heat pan before adding oil or butter for frying.

Salt As A Seasoner ... For cast iron frying pans, instead of washing after each use with soap and water, try shaking salt on the pan and wipe clean. Keeps food from sticking when frying, and needs only to be washed every other day.

- Pancakes won't stick if you rub the griddle with salt first.

Good To The Last Drop! ... Don't pour that last cup of coffee down the drain! Pour it into a thermos bottle and have it later.

- Or, freeze it in ice cube trays for use with iced coffee. The same can apply for tea.

- Always dissolve sugar in a little hot water for use in iced tea and coffee to prevent sugar from sinking to the bottom.

- Try this tasty hint: add a pinch of grated orange rind to tea when steeping for a delicious flavor.

- Coffee beans stay fresh if kept in the freezer compartment of your refrigerator.

Ketchup Too Slow? ... A drinking straw pushed into a slow pouring ketchup bottle will speed up the process. Remove the straw and pour.

Creamier Puddings ... Waxed paper placed over pudding before it has had time to cool will prevent a top layer of film from forming.

Jelly Molds ... Lightly oil the mold and rinse with hot water before using. The mold will lift off easily once gelatin has set.

Uses For Salt Shakers ... Keep a salt shaker filled with flour. It comes in handy when dusting rolling pins or boards.

- Buy spices you use often in bulk and purchase inexpensive salt shakers to store them in.

- Prevent table salt from clogging in the shaker by placing several grains of uncooked rice in the shaker. The rice will absorb excess moisture.

- Keep a salt shaker handy for quick sprinkling while you cook. Combine ¾ salt and ¼ pepper in the same container (or to your own taste).

What To Do With Leftovers

Poultry ... Use your blender and favorite recipe to make a lively pate out of leftover chicken livers.

- Boil leftover chicken or turkey to make a broth that you can store for soups and casseroles later.

Meats ... Add leftover meatloaf to spaghetti sauce.

- Make a meatloaf salad for sandwiches by mixing with onions and mayonnaise.

- Fry up that last piece or two of bacon and crumble for use in salads or as a topping.

- Use ham slices to decorate and liven up muffins. Split centres and stuff with rolled ham. Tasty!

- Dice cooked ham for use in salads or omelettes.

- Slice leftover pork and add to rice dishes or soups.

Pasta ... Add leftover noodles to chicken or beef broth for a delicious 'next day' soup.

- Toss pasta with oil, vegetables and seasonings for a delightful cold noodle salad.

Rice ... Mix with kidney beans, your favorite seasonings and toss. Makes an interesting side dish.

- Add olives and pimentoes for a cold rice salad!

- Turn leftover rice into a pudding!

Tuna ... Leftover tuna salad can be added to cooked macaroni. Sprinkle with cheese and bake for ½ hour. Instant casserole!

Vegetables ... Keep leftover corn, peas, carrots, green beans, etc. for use in a rice salad.

- Make an interesting 'garden' omelette.

- Add to your home made or canned vegetable soup.

- Reheat baked potatoes. Slice at ½ inch intervals and stuff with garlic butter.

- Grated cooked potatoes can be used as a terrific meatloaf extender.

- Pan fry leftover boiled potatoes or boil some eggs and make potato salad.

- Roll mashed potatoes into balls, dip in egg then bread crumbs and bake until golden.

- Try putting leftover salad into the blender. You'll have a delicious gazpacho.

The Wrap Up On Leftovers . . . Did you know plastic wrap won't stick to itself if it's cold.

Freezing Tips

- If you're single and find grocery shopping for one a chore, shop for two and cook for two. Make another serving and freeze in trays for a quick, home made dinner.

- Cooking and freezing extra portions is a great idea for working mothers too, and saves a lot of time doing dishes.

- Don't add salt to hamburger patties intended for the freezer. The salt may create spoilage when combined with fat and shorten its freezer life.

- Add sauce or gravies to cooked meats to avoid drying out in the freezer.

- Avoid using glass bottles with narrow necks for freezing. Fluids expand when frozen and may cause glass to break.

- Iced cakes should be frozen unwrapped to avoid damaging the frosting. As soon as the icing freezes, wrap cake securely and return to freezer.

- Instead of freezing an entire cake or pie, slice, wrap and freeze individual pieces or quarters for use in lunches or dinners for two.

- Be sure to rotate items by date in the freezer to avoid spoilage from stale-dated items.

- The next time you serve waffles or french toast, make extras and freeze them. Reheat in your toaster.

- Freeze leftover coffee in ice cube trays to be used in iced coffee, as a browning agent in gravies, or as a liquid in spice cakes. Once cubes are frozen, remove from tray and place in a plastic bag before returning to freezer.

- Use coffee cans with plastic lids to store goods for the freezer.

- Draw air out of plastic freezer bags by using a straw.

- Keep a package of adhesive backed labels handy for labelling and dating all freezer items.

- When the power goes off, do NOT open the freezer. Cover the freezer with blankets and it should maintain 32°F for up to three days if left unopened.

- If only the freezer power is affected, check the fuse box and plug

TIPS TO MAKE YOUR KITCHEN SPARKLE

Cleaning Up

Can Openers . . . Run a piece of waxed paper through the can opening process to keep it running smoothly.

Blender Cleaning . . . Add a small amount of dishwashing liquid to your blender. Fill half way with hot tap water and blend. Instantly clean!

Electric Mixers & Beaters . . . Prevent messy splatters when using electric mixers by covering the bowl securely with foil. Punch holes in the foil for beaters and beat away!

No More Yellowing . . . Keep white appliances sparkling clean and prevent yellowing by washing with a mixture of ½ cup bleach, 8 cups water, and ½ cup baking soda. Rinse well.

Dishwashers — A Wonderful Invention! . . . The inside of your dishwasher will be film free if you do this occasionally — Fill washer with dirty dishes but make sure you have not included any silver or other metals. Place a bowl with ½ cup bleach on bottom rack and allow the machine to run through the wash cycle only. Fill the same bowl with ½ cup vinegar and this time allow the machine to run a full cycle.

Hot Tips For The Oven . . . When spills occur, sprinkle with table salt. When the oven is cool, wipe up the salt — it will absorb the drippings.

- Avoid oven spills by placing casseroles and pies on a cookie sheet or in a larger pie plate.

- Place a small dish of ammonia on the upper rack and a pan of water on the lower rack of a still warm oven. Leave for 10 to 12 hours or overnight. Air oven and wipe grease away with all-purpose cleaner and warm water. An inexpensive method for oven cleaning.

- Allow oven racks to soak in the tub while you're working on the inside of the oven.

- Rubbing alcohol shines oven tops beautifully.

- Household ammonia diluted with water to half strength makes an excellent oven top cleaner.

Refrigerator Deodorizers ... Freshen up the inside of your refrigerator by wiping periodically with a cloth moistened with vinegar — a great way to prevent mildew.

- A little dab of vanilla, lemon or orange extract on a small pad of cotton will keep the refrigerator smelling sweet.

- Baking soda will keep odors away for several months. Just open the box and place on a middle shelf.

Defrosting ... Defrosting is easier if you wipe the inside of the freezer compartment with a cloth dampened with glycerin. When it's time to defrost again, the chunks of ice will drop without effort.

Instant Kitchen Deodorizer ... Sprinkle cinnamon into a pan of boiling water. The aroma is truly appetizing.

- Lift cooking odors out of the air by placing a few snips of parsley in your cast iron pan. Place over a low heat for five minutes.

- Wintergreen oil dabbed on cotton and placed out of sight keeps rooms sweet smelling.

Enamel Broiling Pans ... Remove tough-to-clean food particles and grease from broiling pans by covering the bottom with a layer of powdered detergent. Cover with a wet dish towel and leave for several hours. This should loosen baked on grease enough to wash without effort.

Plastic Containers ... Eliminate odors by placing ordinary newspaper, crumpled to a ball, inside the container before securing lid. Odors should be gone by morning.

○ Clean stained plastic dishes and utensils by scouring with baking soda.

Rusty Baking Dishes ... Rust can be easily removed from metal baking dishes by scouring with a raw potato and your favorite detergent.

Cast Iron Cookware ... Commercial oven cleaners will clean the OUTSIDE of cast iron cookware. Use as directed but make sure not to use it on the inside. Rinse well after cleaning.

Copper Cleaning ... A little salt and vinegar will clean copper bottoms on pots and pans. Just sprinkle on, rub lightly and wash as usual.

○ Or, rub with a slice of lemon that has been sprinkled with salt.

Thermos Bottles ... Freshen up thermos bottles or insulated coffee pots by filling with warm water mixed with 2 tablespoons baking soda.

Scorched Pans ... Remove as much burnt food as possible from the pan. Sprinkle bottom with baking soda to form a good layer over burnt area. Add 1½ cups water and let stand overnight. Use a rubber spatula to scrape and lift remains.

Fine China ... Tea stains can be removed safely from fine china by rubbing gently with a cloth sprinkled with baking soda or salt.

○ If you have a crack in your fine china plate, place in a pan of warm milk for 15 minutes. The crack should disappear!

○ Place paper doilies or napkins between stacked fine china plates to eliminate scratching.

Crystal & Glassware ... Always slip delicate glassware and crystal into hot water on its side. Place a rubber mat on the bottom of your sink for extra protection against cracking and chipping.

○ Vinegar cleans crystal beautifully. Wash in a mixture of 1 cup white vinegar and 3 cups warm water. Allow to air dry.

○ When two glasses are stuck together, fill the top glass with cold water and submerge the bottom glass in hot water. Gently pull the top glass away.

Graters ... Rub a small amount of salad oil or butter on the grater before using it. Cleaning up is a breeze.

○ Keep a small toothbrush handy to remove foods from your grater.

Kettles ... Clean your kettle periodically by boiling equal parts vinegar and water in it. Let it sit overnight and rinse well in the morning. The lime deposits will wash away.

Sink Drains ... Pouring a solution of hot water and salt (½ cup per quart) into sink drains every other week removes grease and prevents odors.

Porcelain Sink Cleaner ... Porcelain sinks can be cleaned periodically with household bleach. Pour several capfuls over a cloth and run the cloth over the stained areas. Rinse well.

Stainless Steel ... Rubbing alcohol removes spots on stainless steel.

- Clean stainless steel sinks by wiping with a warm soapy cloth. Rinse in hot water. Shine with a dry cloth.

- Remove egg stains on flatware by rubbing with damp salt.

Wooden Boards ... Slice a lemon or lime and rub the board vigorously. Rinse with cold water. Clean and fresh smelling too!

Tricks Of The Trade

Organizers ... Shoe bags are handy when hung in the kitchen closet to hold cords, brushes, whisks and vacuum cleaner attachments.

- Screw a cup hook beside the sink (not over it) to hang rings and watches when washing dishes.

Inexpensive Funnel ... Make a funnel quickly and easily by cutting an empty, clean, plastic bleach or liquid detergent bottle in half. Using the upper half, remove the cap and invert. Be sure to clean thoroughly!

Steel Wool Holder ... Make a decorative holder to keep by the kitchen sink by cutting an empty liquid detergent bottle 2 inches from the bottom, forming a small container. Make a lid to fit by cutting 2 inches from the top of the bottle.

Cleaning Straw Place Mats ... Dissolve 1 cup of salt in a quart of warm water. Wash a section of the mat using a soft brush dipped in the solution. Air dry in the sun before proceeding to the next section.

What...No Corkscrew? ... Place the neck of the wine bottle under hot water for several minutes. The cork should pop out. *For removing wine stains see Laundry Day Helpers p. 73.*

Chilling Beverages... Keep soda and beer cold for your party even though you've run out of refrigerator space. Just fill the top of your washing machine with ice.

Foods That Splatter... A metal colander placed over a frying pan, rim down, will allow steam to escape while eliminating splatters.

A Simple Alarm... You will know when the water boils dry by placing a spoon or jar lid in the bottom pan of your double boiler or steamer. The rattle of the spoon or lid will alert you.

Opening Hard To Open Jars & Bottles... Wear a rubber glove to provide a good grip. It should open easily!

Time Saver... Stock up on ovenproof baking dishes which allow you to go from oven to table without using more dishes and saving time as well.

Your Grocery List... Couponing is the new way to save $$$ galore on your regular grocery bills. Many books are available on the subject and most cities have trader's clubs. Investigate what is available in your area, or start your own. Clip and save as many coupons as you can, trade with friends and neighbors for products you most often buy, and keep a list of what coupons you have to help plan your weekly grocery list.

○ Keep a running grocery list in your purse so you can pick up items you need on your lunch hour or on your way to or from home. Several small shopping jaunts can take less time than one major grocery excursion, and you'll avoid lengthy lineups.

NOTES:

Order
in the House

NOTES:

Plan Ahead

- Clean one room at a time. If you are interrupted, at least one room is finished and you can continue cleaning later.

- When cleaning around the house, carry a bucket or basket filled with all the cleaning materials you need for any given room. This eliminates trips back and forth, and saves time.

- Put on your leotards or exercise outfit when cleaning. The psychological effect will make all that bending and lifting seem like exercise instead of work.

All About Cleaning Furniture

Polishers & Cleaners... A great home-made polish can be made from equal parts of vinegar, turpentine and linseed oil. Bottle it and shake well before using. Apply with a soft cloth and polish with another clean cloth.

- Or, mix one part lemon juice to two parts olive or vegetable oil for another great polisher.

Instant Cleaning Mitts... Use old woolen or terry socks as dusters.

- Or, sew a pair of mitts out of an old hand towel. Great for cleaning venetian blinds because you can clean both sides of the slat with one movement.

Applying Extra Elbow Grease... Getting a perfect shine is sometimes tough work. Try wrapping a brick or heavy piece of wood with your buffing cloth. The extra weight means you won't have to press as hard.

Dust Cloth Treatment... Dip cheesecloth squares in a mixture of ½ cup lemon oil and 1 pint hot water. Squeeze out excess moisture and dry thoroughly. Store cloths in clean coffee cans with secure lids.

Getting Rid Of Sticky Marks... Here's a good home made furniture cleaner for wiping up sticky marks. Mix 1 tablespoon turpentine, and 3 tablespoons linseed oil to a quart of hot water. Mix well and allow to cool. Wring a soft cloth in the solution and wipe where needed. Dry at once with a clean soft cloth and rub to polish.

White Spots... Remove white spots on mahogany by covering the spot with a thick layer of petroleum jelly. Wait 48 hours before wiping off.

Water Rings ... Try applying a paste of cooking oil and salt. Wait 15 minutes and wipe off. Polish as usual.

- Or, apply a small amount of toothpaste and baking soda to a damp cloth and rub the stain lightly.

Remember ... Don't polish any wooden surface when it is damp or white patches may appear.

- Place a small piece of waxed paper under clay pots to save wooden surfaces.

Remedy For Greying Wood Surfaces ... When a whitish-grey film appears on wood furniture, mix a small amount of vinegar (1-2 tbsp) with a pint of water and soak a soft cloth in it. Wring the cloth lightly and let remaining mixture in the cloth drip onto the wood surface. Rub lightly. If this solution doesn't take, sanding may be required.

Burns On Wooden Furniture ... Combine vegetable oil with rottenstone (available at hardware stores) to make a paste. Apply to burned area only, rubbing gently into the grain. Wipe clean and polish as usual.

Did You Know ... If you keep any wood furniture too near a heat source it may crack or warp. Alternatively if you keep furniture in a damp atmosphere it may swell making drawers difficult to open. For the latter, try using a little soap along drawer runners for a smooth glide.

Unsticking Paper From Wood ... Try soaking the paper in cooking oil for a few minutes. Rub with a cloth to 'roll' paper off.

Home-Made Polish Remover ... A solution of equal parts vinegar and water will serve as an economical polish remover. Moisten a cloth with the solution and wipe until dry.

Treating Heat Marks ... Remove heat marks from varnished or shellacked wood surfaces by dabbing spirits of camphor on the spot with a soft cloth. Allow to dry and then polish.

- For lacquered wood surfaces, apply a paste of powdered pumice and linseed oil. Rub in direction of the grain, and polish.

Reaching Those Tiny Crevices ... To clean tiny crevices in carved furniture, use a cotton-wrapped orange stick or cotton swab.

Or, spray the bristles of an artist's paint brush with furniture polish to dust and polish at the same time.

Invisible Scratches ... conceal scratches in dark wood by dyeing the scratch with iodine. For lighter wood rub with the cut surface of walnut or brazil nut meat.

- Crayons also work well. Select the right color and melt a small amount. Work the melted wax into the scratch or nick until concealed.

Especially For Antiques ... Mix a solution of 2 parts turpentine to 1 part linseed oil, or use equal parts turpentine with linseed oil and vinegar. Apply with a soft cloth and rub with another clean soft cloth to polish.

How To 'Raise Cane' ... Tighten up sagging cane seats by sponging both sides with hot soapy water to which you've added a few spoonfuls of salt. Rinse with a clean wet cloth and allow to dry in the sun. When almost dry, cover caning with a towel and run a hot iron over it.

Do's & Don'ts For Wicker Furniture ... Don't leave wicker outside in freezing weather. The coldness will cause wicker to become brittle and split.

- Wicker furniture requires moisture to prevent dryness, so turn the humidifier on occasionally, especially during winter months.

- Clean wicker furniture by scrubbing with a stiff brush dipped in warm salt water. The salt prevents wicker from yellowing.

Leather Furniture ... Keep leather supple by polishing every month with a solution of 2 parts linseed oil and 1 part vinegar.

- Saddle soap cleans leather beautifully.

What To Do About Grease Stains On Upholstery ... Sprinkle liberally with salt as soon as the accident occurs. Allow salt to absorb grease before brushing away.

Blood Stains ... As soon as possible, cover blood stain with a paste of cornstarch and water. Allow to dry and brush off. Repeat again if necessary.

Shining Plastic Furniture ... Apply a small amount of toothpaste to the plastic surface and rub in. Buff with a clean cloth. This tip helps remove scratches from plastic as well.

Getting The 'Royal Carpet' Treatment

Sounds Corny, But ... You'll liven up a solid, light colored carpet by brushing in cornmeal before vacuuming.

Homemade Carpet Shampoo... Use ½ cup powder detergent, 1 tsp. ammonia, and a quart of warm water. Mix all ingredients in a bowl, stirring constantly to work up a layer of froth. Using froth only, rub lightly with a sponge or cloth over the entire carpet. When necessary, continue stirring solution to get additional froth. Allow carpet to dry. Vacuum entire area.

Protecting Furniture During The Shampoo... Keep furniture legs free from damage when shampooing the carpet by slipping plastic baggies over the legs. This will also protect your carpet from rust stains caused by metal legs, and from smudges from dampened furniture oil.

When The Glue Is On The Wrong Side Of The Carpet... remove it by pressing the spot firmly with a cloth that has been dipped in vinegar.

A Carpet That Curls?... Try cutting a triangle of tile or linoleum and applying to the underside of each curled corner using double-sided carpet tape.

Frayed Carpet... Instead of fretting over a fraying braided carpet, glue the pieces together with fabric glue.

Raising The Pile... Raise the flattened carpet pile by holding a steam iron over the area. Allow steam to penetrate pile, and brush the spot immediately. Remember not to touch the carpet with the iron.

- Dampen a chamois and fold several times. Place it over the flattened nap and leave for several hours. The nap should lift right up.

Removing Carpet Stains... If the carpet stain is still wet, try pouring a little club soda on the stained area. Wait a moment, and blot until moisture is absorbed.

- If you don't find the stain right away, mix a diluted solution of vinegar, soap and water. Dampen a cloth with this solution and press firmly against stain for several moments. Blot dry with a rinse cloth.

- Never rub a carpet to soak up liquid that has been spilled. Using as much dry cloth as you need, blot the area until most of the liquid has been absorbed. But don't rub it in!

- Shaving cream is a terrific instant carpet stain remover.

- Salt is also a great pepper-upper for tired carpets and is a terrific absorbing agent for mud stains. Sprinkle it liberally on fresh stain and allow to soak up moisture. Then vacuum.

○ Or sprinkle it all over your carpet, vacuum, and smile at the results!

Homemade Carpet Stain Remover... Add 1 tsp. of vinegar to a pint of Homemade Carpet Shampoo (see pg. 30) and mix together to form a lather. Rub stain gently with a lathered sponge and rinse the area with clear water.

Cigarette Burns... Snip away the singed edges with fine manicure scissors or a razor blade. If it's still noticeable, remove several strands of carpet yarn from another area. Use tweezers to pull out the severely burned fibers and discard. Apply glue to the burned area and press down the clean fibers into the spot. Place a heavy object, such as a hassock, over the burned area and allow several days to dry completely.

Throw Rugs That Throw You... Use rubber rings from preserve jars to end sliding rugs. Glue three together and then glue to each corner. The rings will form a suction cup to help keep the mat in its place, and you in yours!

Carpet Sweepers & Beaters... To remove thread wound around the rotating brush, slice threads with scissors and pull shortened threads out.

○ For non-electric carpet sweepers, try wetting the bristles to help pick up lint more quickly.

Hints For Floors, Walls & Woodwork

Prevent Scratched Floors... Slip a small scatter rug under heavy dressers and place old socks on furniture legs when rearranging a room.

○ Prevent marring on wooden floors by placing a long strip of adhesive tape along the bottom of each arc of your rocking chair.

○ Or, glue strips of felt to the arc bottoms.

Removing The Scratch... Remove scratches in wooden floors by sanding very gently with fine steel wool that has been dipped in paste wax.

Polisher Pad Buildup... Remove excess wax build-up by placing brown paper over pads and pressing with a warm iron. The wax will melt and adhere to the brown paper.

Crayon Marks... Remove wax crayon marks from vinyl or linoleum flooring by rubbing with silver polish.

Linoleum ... Linoleum floors should never be scrubbed with abrasive cleansers or cleaning tools. Simply wash with a wet mop that has been dipped in warm, soapy water. Wring well.

- When sweeping up, dip the tip of your broom in water to help pick up dust.

Registers & Vents ... Place a piece of screening inside floor vents and registers to catch small objects that fall and dust that collects.

Cleaning Woodwork ... Squeeze the juice of one lemon into one quart of water for use as a rinse after washing woodwork or linoleum. The surfaces will maintain their high gloss finish.

- Use cold tea to clean woodwork.

Removing Candlewax From Woodwork ... The trick is to soften the wax enough to wipe it up with an absorbent cloth. Try using a hair dryer. Wash woodwork afterward with a mild vinegar solution to remove all traces of wax.

A Swell Tip ... If your wooden doors expand and seem impossible to close, check the position of your humidifier. Wood absorbs moisture and swells slightly.

No Streaking, Please! ... When washing painted walls, always start at the bottom and work your way up. This prevents streaks from dripping water that are difficult to remove.

Wallpaper ... Cleaning marks on wallpaper is easy if you rub the stain with rye bread or an artgum eraser
Also see Home & Car Maintenance pg. 46.

Drapery Ideas

Which One Goes Where? ... Mark your drapery panels before they go to the cleaners so you'll know exactly where they belong when returned home. On the underside of the individual panel hems, place a single long stitch in contrasting thread on the panel closest to the left side of the window. Increase by one stitch for every panel, moving in a counter clockwise rotation around the room.

- Mark the location of drapery hooks with a dab of coloured nail polish when removing them. The polish will remain throughout the dry cleaning process and will make reinserting the hooks a simple task.

Hooks & Weights ... Drapery hooks are inserted easily into fabric if you first push the pointed end of the hook into a soap bar.

- ○ Use old keys as drapery weights.

- ○ Or, raid the tool box for several heavy 'nuts' to use as weights.

Hints For Windows

When To Wash Windows... Wait for a cloudy day to wash normally 'sunny' windows. The sun will cause the glass to dry too quickly, leaving unsightly streaks.

The Final Shine... Keep a lambswool mop pad in your cleaning basket to be used for giving glass a final buffing.

Save On Paper Towelling... Use crumpled newspaper to dry windows.

Homemade Window Cleaner... Mix ¼ cup white vinegar and ¼ cup ammonia into a bucket half filled with warm water. Fill several spray bottles or plant misters and you'll have an excellent cleaner, as well as a long lasting supply.

- ○ To give your homemade window cleaner a 'professional' appeal, try adding a drop of blue food coloring to each container and shake well.

Frost Free Windows... Add 2 tbl. of rubbing alcohol to a container of "Homemade Window Cleaner" to help prevent frost forming on the inside windows.

Cleaning Screens... Use a soft paint brush to dust screens before cleaning.

- ○ Dip paint brush in kerosene and brush both sides of the screen. Dry with a clean cloth.

Cleaning The Bathroom

Keeping The Bathroom Tidy... If your family bathroom seems to self-destruct daily, try this idea. Give each member of the family a towel rack of their own. Assign certain towels for each person to use (favorite colors is the easiest way). Presto! No more second-guessing when about to dry your face, and you'll be pleasantly surprised at the decreased laundry load.

Shower Curtains... Soap film is quickly and easily removed from plastic shower curtains. Place several large bath towels in the washing machine along with the shower curtain. Add ½ cup of baking soda along with ½ cup powdered detergent and allow machine to run through wash cycle using warm water. When machine is filling with rinse water, add ½ cup vinegar. Remove curtain before spin cycle and hang immediately.

Cleaning Bathroom Tile ... Mix a solution of 1 cup ammonia, 1 cup vinegar with ½ cup washing soda in a bucket of warm water. Wash down the tiles and rinse thoroughly.

- For quick rinsing, try running the hot shower for a few moments with the bathroom door closed. The steam will form beads of water that can easily be dried with a soft cloth.

Instant Towel Rack ... Make use of that old wine rack in the bathroom. Roll up towels and place in bottle slots for a creative and decorative touch.

Keeping Soap Dishes Clean ... Try cutting a sponge approx. ½ inch thick to fit the inside of your soap dish. The sponge will soak up any water left on the bar of soap, and prevent slimy build up. Rinse the sponge every other day.

Stains In The Bathtub ... Mix a paste of lemon juice and borax and apply to badly stained sink or bathtub.

- Remove old yellow water stains by rubbing with a mixture of salt and turpentine.

- Badly stained tubs need a special treatment. Scrub well with a scrub brush dipped in a mixture of cream of tartar and peroxide.

Toilet Rings ... Remove toilet rings with a paste of lemon juice and borax. Allow to set before scrubbing away.

- For removing very old and stubborn toilet stains pour ½ cup of "Vanish" crystals into the bowl and leave overnight. Excessively stained bowls might require several applications.

Bathtub Decals ... Bathtub decals are great, unless you want them removed. Try soaking in mineral spirits and scrape until the decals are lifted. Sprinkle with cleanser and scrub with an abrasive pad to remove glue. Once this is done, you will have to bring the shine back on the enamel. Wax entire tub with Turtle Wax, and shine with a dry cloth.

Cloggy Showerheads ... Remove lime deposits from showerheads by removing head and bringing to boil in a mixture of equal parts vinegar and water.

Preventive Plumbing ... Pouring a solution of water and salt (½ cup salt per quart of water) into sink drains every other week removes grease and prevents odors.

Around The House:

Chrome ... Dampen a cloth with ammonia to clean and shine chrome in a single step.

Silver Cleaner ... Use this easy and quick method to clean solid silver that has not been oxidized previously. In an aluminum pan (or pan covered with aluminum foil) add 1 tblsp. soda and 1 tblsp. salt to a quart of water. Set silver to be cleaned in the pan making sure it touches the aluminum. Bring to a boil and remove immediately (do not allow to remain boiling). Wash, rinse, and dry silver. The aluminum pan may discolor requiring a treatment of 1 tblsp. cream of tartar boiled in a quart of water.

Piano Keys ... Rub with a lemon half to clean the surface. Or use a paste of salt and lemon juice. Wipe with a clean cloth.

- Or, clean with a cloth moistened slightly with denatured alcohol. Wipe dry.

- Remember, never use soap to clean ivory. It will definitely stain.

Gilt Frames ... Be gentle please! The first thing to remember when cleaning gilt frames is to pat on the cleaner, never rub. Start by mixing together equal parts of ammonia and denatured alcohol. Dampen a soft cloth with this solution and apply to a small area of the frame, dabbing gently. Next dab the area with a dry soft cloth to pick up the dirt. Continue until entire frame has been cleaned.

Gilt Frame Preserver ... Twice each year, apply a small amount of lemon oil to frames to prevent cracking.

Pewter ... Clean pewter by rubbing with cabbage leaves.

Vases ... Add a capful of ammonia and fill vase with hot water. Rinse thoroughly.

Artificial Plants & Flowers ... Clean by spraying with an all-purpose cleanser and rinsing in warm water.

- Or, clean artificial flower centerpieces by holding the container and dunking in warm soapy water, then clear water. Let it sit upside down on a towel until moisture has run off.

Mopping Up ... Here's a 'pollution' wise method for shaking mops. Place a plastic or paper bag over the mophead and secure with a twist tie or elastic. Shake vigorously and discard the bag filled with dust. Especially useful for apartment dwellers.

Tobacco Smoke ... Burn several decorative candles to lift smoke.

○ Activated charcoal will also remove stale smoke odors. Place small amounts in saucers around the room.

Cleaning Silk Lamp Shades ... Before cleaning, check for color fastness and to ensure that glue was not used to affix trimming. Working quickly, dip the shade up and down in soapy lukewarm water. Use a soft brush on stained areas. Rinse several times. Towel sponge until most moisture is removed. Do not place in the sun or near heat, but dry in a well-ventilated, shaded area. Turn upside down to even drying process occasionally. Remember the trick is to dry the shade as quickly as possible without using heat.

Dusty Radiators ... Hang a damp tea towel behind the radiator and use your blow dryer to blow the dust onto the towel.

Porcelain ... Clean porcelain by rubbing with a soft cloth sprinkled with salt.

Removing Stains From Marble ... Scrub with a paste of baking soda, water, and a few drops of lemon juice. Rinse and dry.

Fireplaces ... Happiness is a roaring fire on a cold night, but unhappiness is trying to keep the hearth clean. Try sprinkling salt over logs to remove up to 75% of the soot.

○ Keep an artgum eraser handy for removing soot on stone fireplace fronts. If discoloring remains use a solution of trisodium phosphate and water (1 oz. per quart).

○ For really big jobs, get prepared by sweeping all the dead ashes up and then vacuuming thoroughly. Place newspapers around and inside the hearth. Don your rubber gloves and get set. Make sure you have on hand a bucket of clear water, a cloth, a bowl of vinegar, and a scrub brush. Dip the brush in vinegar and scrub a section of tile. Rinse and wipe with cloth and water. Continue until all sections have been cleaned.

Crystal Chandeliers ... Place a plastic cover over the table along with a few layers of newspapers. Fill a glass with lukewarm water and add 2 oz. alcohol or vinegar. Hold the glass up to the individual crystal teardrops until totally immersed. Let them drip dry.

Candles ... Keep spare candles in the refrigerator. They'll burn slowly and evenly if cold.

○ Candlewax can be removed from silver holders. Try refrigerating the holders until wax is easily chipped off.

◦ Remove wax drippings or splatters by placing a blotter, or plain brown paper, over the area. Press a warm iron, or a warm pan of water, onto the paper. The wax will melt and stick to the paper.

◦ Prevent an accident from occurring. If your candle holder is too large for the candle you have, melt some paraffin and fill the socket. Before it hardens, insert the too-small candle.

Books & Bindings... Keep books away from radiators or strong sunlight. The heat will warp covers and excessive light will fade bindings.

◦ Don't jam books too tightly on shelves or bindings may break from the pressure.

◦ Books should be stored in an upright position, never leaning to one side. If the book is too tall for the shelf, lay it flat. Use bookends to hold books upright.

Playing Cards With A Full Deck... Old playing cards can be rejuvenated by applying a little spirits of camphor dabbed lightly with cotton balls. Just wipe and polish.

Avoiding Closet Dampness... Place a box of chalk on the shelf of your closet to eliminate dampness.

◦ Charcoal also absorbs dampness. Place in a container that has several air holes in it and set it on the floor of the closet.

Removing Gum From Clothes, Carpets, Shoes, Etc... Hold an ice cube against the chewing gum until frozen. Chip gum away. *Also see Laundry Day Helpers pg. 73.*

Hints For The Exterminator

Ants... Sage will repel ants. Sprinkle around affected areas, in crevices, and in cupboards.

◦ Or, boil one pint of tar in 2 quarts of water. Set in an uncovered dish where ants gather.

Cockroaches... Boric acid is an effective way to eliminate cockroaches. It may take some time to be rid of them, but it will do the job. Sprinkle in cracks and trouble areas, and leave the container open in the cupboard.

Hornets and Bees... Use hairspray to stop bees or hornets in action. Pour hot water down crevices and where you suspect hornets are nesting.

- If numerous, place a glass jug with a small opening outside your door or where you suspect they congregate. Fill the jug half way with water and smear honey or fruit juice along the rim and inside the opening. The bees will gather here and drown in the water. Unpleasant but effective.

- If the bee is inside the house, turn the lights off and turn the patio light on. The bee will fly to the light.

Garbage Raiders ... Keep a spray bottle filled with turpentine or ammonia and spray garbage bags and pails lightly to repel animals from raiding the garbage and leaving you with a mess to clean up.

Crawling Bugs ... Depart quickly when baseboards walls and cracks are painted with a mixture of 3 quarts boiled water with 2 tblsp. alum.

- Leave a cotton wad dampened with oil of pennyroyal where spiders reside. They'll flee quickly.

Flying Bugs ... Flying bugs hate smoke, so light an incense stick or candle to drive them away.

Flies ... Leave a dish of molasses and black pepper where they congregate.

Moths ... Darken the room and leave a bright light burning outside. They'll fly to the light.

- Hang sachets of cedarwood chips in closets to keep them away.

Mosquitoes ... They dislike the scent of oil of pennyroyal so rub on your skin when they're around. Mosquitoes like damp clothing and strangely enough, the color blue.

Fleas ... Soak cotton cording in oil of pennyroyal and tie loosely around your pet's collar. Change every other week.

- Keep sachets of camomile leaves in the 'doghouse' to help drive fleas away.

Dog About The House

I Want My Mother! ... Little puppies and kittens need motherly love and warmth. Place a warm hot water bottle securely under his blanket along with a ticking clock for those first few nights.

Oops, Another Accident! ... Soda water will remove the odor from accidents caused by untrained pups. Gently rub the area with a cloth dampened with soda water. This is especially good on fabrics.

Beware Of Driver! ... Paint an inexpensive dog tag with irridescent paint and attach to your pet's collar. This will enable drivers to see him at night.

○ Or, put a hole in a small plastic bicycle reflector and attach to his collar.

○ Cut small pieces of reflector tape and apply to both sides of a dog tag. Affix to collar with other tags.

Something Smells ... Animals dislike perfume odors on their coats. Use only odorless 'animal' shampoos or soaps when bathing.

Removing Burrs ... Using work gloves, work baby oil into coat areas tangled by burrs. This should loosen the 'grip' enough to free burrs.

Skunked Again! ... Get out the tomato juice and douse your pet thoroughly. Shampoo and add a few drops of lemon juice to the rinse water. Be sure to rinse well.

Dry Shampoo ... Give your pet an occasional 'dry' shampoo. Rub in baking soda and brush his coat until soda has been swept away along with the dirt. This is an especially safe way of keeping him clean during the cold winter months.

Fleas ... See Hints For The Exterminator pg. 38.

NOTES:

NOTES:

THE HANDYPERSON

Tools & Workshops

Your Tool Box ... Minimum suggested contents.

- Hammer with a curved claw back for pulling nails.
- Two screwdrivers — one small and one medium.
- Tape measure, 10ft. retractable.
- Carpenter's level (to get things straight).
- Electric drill — 3/8" with accessories.
- Heavy canvas working gloves.
- A flashlight.
- Pliers.
- A putty knife.
- Electrical tape.
- An adjustable wrench.
- Assorted nails and screws.
- Plunger.
- A pencil — you can never find one when you need it.

- Most hand tools last a lifetime but it's well worth investing in high quality equipment. They will make difficult tasks simpler and save hours of frustration.

Tricks Of The Tool Trade ... In an emergency a large nail will sometimes act as a Phillips screwdriver.

- If you store small hand tools in a damp basement, try putting a few mothballs in the toolbox to absorb moisture.

- Nylon rope that has been cut should have the raw end heated to prevent fraying. Ordinary rope can be dipped in shellac or verathane.

- Rusty garden tools are easily cleaned by rubbing with a soap-filled steel wool pad. Dip the pad in turpentine and rub vigorously.

- Prevent small garden tools from rusting by immersing them in a bucket of sand kept in the garden or toolshed.

- Self-polishing floor wax works wonders to protect household tools from rust. Simply coat the metal or cutting blade with wax and allow to dry.

- Multi-leveled cardboard storage containers are commonly available at office supply stores. They are excellent for organizing the various grades of sandpaper you keep in the workshop.

- Don't throw that piece of sandpaper away just because it feels smooth. Sandpaper often becomes clogged, but can easily be cleared by a fine bristle shoe brush.

- Sanding large flat areas is easier and more even if you wrap the sandpaper around a block of wood that fits easily into your hand.

- Get to know your local hardware store owner. They know absolutely everything and can not only provide all sorts of free advice, but also the occasional miracle tool that makes an impossible job simple.

Tips For The Painter

- Your house should be painted every three to five years. Paint the north and west sides in the morning and the south and east sides in the afternoon.

- Wet paint appears to have a different color than dry paint. To make a quick comparison of a freshly mixed color, paint a small piece of metal and dry it in the oven or on the radiator.

- Be Careful! Even odorless paints produce fumes that are dangerous to your health if inhaled — especially with alcohol in your system. Save the celebration until after you've finished painting.

- If you're using a roller, line the pan with a plastic garbage bag before pouring in the paint. Clean up time will be reduced considerably.

- Old paint brushes can be made new by soaking in hot vinegar.

- Old paint sometimes gets lumpy. A piece of wire mesh cut to fit inside the can will sink to the bottom carrying the lumps with it.

- Apply petroleum jelly on brass hinges, doorknobs, and any other hardware you don't want painted. It might also be a good idea to rub the back of your hands and face with it to make washing up a simpler matter.

- Pour paint into an old coffee mug. It's much easier to handle for small painting jobs.

- Don't be a drip! If you have ever had paint drip from the handle of a brush and down your arm, try sticking the handle of the brush through the center of a paper plate.

Painting Windows... Rub soft bar soap around window edges to avoid painting glass.

○ Make sure you clean all the dirt out of difficult-to-reach corners and edges before painting. Try using an artist's long-handled paint brush to sweep it out.

○ Strips of writing paper soaked in warm water and placed snugly around the edges of the glass will stay in place long enough for you to paint the window frame.

Putty In Your Hands... Save hours touching up new putty around your windows by mixing in paint — the same color as your window frames — before installing.

Too Late To Finish... Even the best planners find themselves with a half-finished job at midnight. If it's too late or you don't have time to thoroughly clean paint brushes, try storing them in plastic sandwich bags overnight. Secure with an elastic band around the handle.

Cleaning Up... When you've finished painting, mark the level of paint remaining in the can on the outside before cleaning your brush.

○ When replacing the lid on old paint or shellac cans you'll want a tight fit. Before tapping the lid with your hammer, place an old rag over the can to catch excess paint that has accumulated in the groove around the lip of the can.

○ Leave a pail of water inside a freshly painted room and the odor will disappear quickly.

○ Paint thinner is reusable. Allow the container you've used to clean your brushes to sit for a few days. After the paint has settled to the bottom, pour the thinner into a clean container.

○ You know you saved those small glass containers (aspirin jars, jam jars, etc.) for something. Use them for leftover paint and quick touch-ups.

Removing Paint Splatters On Skin... Cooking oil will remove most paint from skin without the irritation caused by some commercial products.

Paint Stains... Turpentine will work on paint stains. Just soak and scrape with an old putty knife or razor blade.

○ Vinegar and water will remove newly dried paint from glass surfaces.

○ Apply nail polish remover to old paint splatters on windows. Wait a few minutes and wash off, rubbing lightly.

Finding The Wall Stud ... Wall studs (floor to ceiling lengths of 2 x 4s) are usually located 16″ apart. If you start in the corner and measure 17″ you should hit the centre of the first stud. Be careful, electrical wires often run through the centre of studs.

Avoid Cracking Plaster ... Place a small piece of tape over the spot on the wall you plan to nail.

Concrete Walls ... If you have concrete walls, which are often covered with plaster or thin wallboard, forget nails. Get out the electric drill and be sure to have a vairety of plugs (metal and plastic) on hand to hold the screws you'll need to hold things up.

Wallpaper ... Grease spots can be lightened and often removed by applying a mixture of cornstarch and water. Allow mixture to dry, then brush away. Repeat if necessary.

- ○ To prevent grease spots on old wallpaper from soaking through to new paper, paint the spots with shellac first.

- ○ Joins and edges of wallpaper tend to peel, especially in the bathroom and kitchen. Try painting with a small amount of clear shellac.

- ○ Believe it or not, soft chunks of stale bread rubbed over wallpaper in long vertical strokes will remove soiled spots.

- ○ Peeling wallpaper can be reglued. Using wallpaper paste, smear on a piece of writing paper using a kitchen knife. Blot excess. Working from the point closest to the intact wallpaper, rub pasted paper against the underside of the unglued wallpaper. Hold paper against wallpaper for a moment. Then tear the writing paper away and press the wallpaper against the wall. Smooth away any air bubbles.

- ○ When getting ready to wallpaper — start straight! Don't trust room corners. Suspend a chalked and weighted piece of string from a high point on the wall. When it comes to rest, pull it taut against the baseboard. Snap the string at the center. The mark it leaves will be a true vertical.

Measuring For Wallpaper ... Here's a formula for determining how many rolls you'll need to cover any room in your house. Measure the height of the ceiling (floor to ceiling measurement). Measure the length of two walls and the width of two walls. Total the lengths and widths and multiply by the ceiling height. Divide this total by 30. Example: The room is 10′ x 12′ and the ceiling is 8′ high. The total lengths and widths is (10' + 10' + 12' + 12') 44'. Multiply 44' by the ceiling height of 8' to arrive at 352. Divide 352 by 30 to get 11 2/3 single rolls. You can deduct one single roll for every two openings such as a door or window, however, after making all calculations and deductions, add one roll for safety.

Panelling ... Even the most careful handyperson will find annoying white spaces between wall panels. Try spraying black paint on the blackboard before applications of panels.

○ Water tends to discolor wood panelling. It may sound insane, but cover the light spot with mayonnaise at night and by morning the stain will have disappeared.

○ When a switch box requires a cut out in the panel — place the panel in its normal position over the box. Lay a soft wood block over the approximate location. Tap the block soundly. The outlet box will make its imprint on the back of the panel for easy and accurate cutting.

Finishing The Basement ... Before application of panelling, check walls for excessive moisture. Failure to seal off moisture can cause molding, warping; separation, and discoloration.

○ To test for condensation on basement walls, place a small mirror against the wall. If droplets or fog appear you'll need to seal the wall. Permit walls to dry before applying panelling.

Sticky Windows ... Beeswax on the pulley stiles will make the window glide easily up and down.

Sweaty Windows ... If sweating occurs on the inside window, the storm is not properly sealed. If sweating occurs on the storm window, the inside window is leaking.

Floors & Doors

Squeaks, Rattles, And Things That Go Bump In The Night ... Oil everything that squeaks except floors and complicated mechanisms like tumbler locks. Squeaky floor boards should be nailed at an angle with the heads of the nails punched just below the surface of the wood.

○ Gouges in resilient flooring can be repaired. Shave a little floor covering from a matching scrap or an inconspicuous tile. Mix scrapings with clear lacquer and apply with a putty knife.

○ Remember to remove old nails and staples before applying tile to an old floor.

- If floors creak, try sprinkling the area with talcum powder. Rub in lightly and sweep remaining powder away.

Knobs & Hinges ... Doorknobs that rattle are usually fixed easily by tightening a tiny set screw just behind the handle. If this doesn't work, you may have to replace the spindle that goes through the hole in the door.

- If hinges still squeak after oiling, remove and clean with steel wool. Remember to do one hinge at a time and avoid the awkward job of rehanging a door.

- Rusty bolts are best lubricated by using a penetrating oil, but in a pinch try applying liberal amounts of carbonated soda water.

Tips For The Carpenter

Carpenter's Golden Rule ... Measure twice, cut once.

- Prevent splitting plywood by starting the cut with a fine-toothed saw.

- Even newly purchased lumber is rarely squared. Always check corners before measuring.

- If you need small odds and ends of wood to complete a minor repair, ask your local lumber dealer if you can look through his 'scrap box'.

- Top and bottom surfaces of plywood are rated as either A, B or C, depending on the appearance of the wood. A/A finish would have smooth, well-finished wood on both sides. A/C would have one smooth surface and one coarse surface, and of course would cost less.

- Remember, when using a handsaw always saw from the finished side, and when using a powersaw, saw from the unfinished side.

Repairing & Refinishing Furniture ... If you are rebuilding old furniture, loosen glued joints by applying nail polish remover from a small oil can.

- When stripping, place aluminum pie plates under the legs of tables and chairs to catch drippings. Saves on clean up time, prevents potential damage to working surface, and economizes on expensive stripper.

- Try a homemade stain for furniture — strong tea.

- Many stains are very thin and unless you have very large brushes, you'll be working for hours on those large, flat surfaces. Try using a sponge instead, but be sure to wear rubber gloves.

- Wobbly furniture drawers can be reinforced with small triangular wood blocks glued and nailed into the corners.

- Don't force sticky drawers. Rub the edges with hard soap or wax. If that doesn't work, try sanding the drawer edges lightly.

- Lighten spots or stains in old furniture by using laundry bleach. Bleach the spot bit by bit with multiple applications.

- Keep vinegar or borax handy when applying bleach to furniture. You can stop the action of bleach as soon as the wood reaches the correct tone.

- Wax sticks are terrific for repairing minor furniture scratches, but keeping track of them can be a problem. Try taping the wax stick that matches your table to the underside so that it's there when you need it.

- When painting or refinishing anything with legs, hammer a small nail or tack in the bottom of each leg and avoid sticky paper residue.

- Large gouges in furniture can be repaired by sanding an inconspicuous surface of the piece to be repaired. Mix the sawdust with white glue and apply the paste to the damaged area.

Hung Up On A Picture Frame... When measuring to hang pictures, remember to take into account how many inches the wire sags under the weight of the picture.

Tips For The Electrician

Fuses... Fuses protect your electrical system from overloading. One too many appliances drawing electricity can cause the wires to heat, and without fuses, can start a fire inside the walls. Replace blown fuses with the same size fuse, and if necessary unplug one or more appliances.

- Know what's where — a good rainy day activity. Turn on electrical appliances in the house. Go to the fuse box and; remove one fuse. Note which appliances stop working. Repeat with each and every fuse and keep the record in the fuse box for future reference.

- Always test an electrical circuit before beginning work. A voltage tester is simply two wires with a little bulb between them. Make sure you periodically check your voltage tester in a circuit that does work so that you are sure it's operating.

- It is possible for old toast crumbs in a toaster to conduct electricity from the heating wire to the metal cases. Remember to clean the toaster and never poke anything in the toaster while it is plugged in.

- An inexpensive pencil flashlight clipped to the handle of your fusebox will save problems in the event of a power failure.

- If you get tired of buying fuses, it is possible to replace them with individual circuit breakers.

- Large appliances usually have their own "cartridge" fuse. Be sure to remove these only with a "fuse puller", and preferably with the main power switch off.

- Thin wire in a long extension cord drains electrical power. It can significantly reduce power to an electric heater and even your electrical drill will turn more slowly if its at the end of a long extension cord.

Cords & Cables ... Remember to unplug any electrical appliance you are working on.

- Electrical extension cords can be kept tangle free by winding the cord and inserting into a cardboard roll. Write the length of the cord on the outside of the tube.

- When cutting electric cable, be sure to add 20% to your straight line measurement. Cable does not bend easily or lie perfectly flat.

- If you're attaching plastic sheathed cables with staples, be careful not to drive the staple too far or you may cause a short in the cable.

Fluorescent Lights ... All fluorescent lights generate a hum. They are rated from low noise level (A) to a high, annoying level (F). Be sure to check the noise level before you buy.

Lampwires ... Never run lamp wires under carpet. Eventually ridges are worn into the fabric and you may have a potential fire hazard underfoot.

Soldering ... When you solder a fitting that is situated close to wood, always put a sheet of asbestos behind the fitting to stop the flame. Carry a dry chemical fire extinguisher with you whenever you solder.

Small Motors ... Small appliances often have fan blades to force air past the motor. Heat can destroy motors so make sure ventilation is available.

Reducing Noise Pollution ... Reduce noise by placing major appliances that vibrate such as washing machines, dryers, refrigerators etc. on resilient pads.This also facilitates easy movement across tile floors.

Pipes & Plumbing

Frozen Pipes ... If they aren't frozen too badly, try turning the faucets upside down with a wrench then pouring a gallon of boiling salted water down the faucet.

- Frozen pipes can sometimes be rescued by a hairdryer.

- Always start near an open valve or faucet when heating a frozen pipe. This allows steam to escape harmlessly. Never let the pipe get too hot to touch with your hands.

- Know where the main valve that brings water to your house is and know how to shut it off. In the event of a broken water pipe, this will be your first action. Finding and correcting the leak can then proceed. If the leak is in the hot water system, turn off the electricity to the hot water heater, and if your house is heated by water, the boiler.

- If you must tighten exposed plumbing pipes, wrap them first with two or three layers of plastic electrical tape to protect them from wrench teeth.

Faucets — Nobody Likes A Drip ... Solve your problem with these easy steps:

1. Turn off water under sink or at source.
2. Open faucet to drain water.
3. Unscrew faucet handle.
4. Unscrew nut that holds faucet stem in place with an adjustable wrench.
5. Pull out faucet stem.
6. Remove screw at bottom which holds washer.
7. Remove washer and replace with same size new washer.
8. Repeat above steps in reverse order.

- If a leaking faucet keeps you awake during the night, try tying a piece of cotton string or cording to the tap so that the water will run the length of the cord right into the drain. Make a mental note to fix it tomorrow, and get a good night's rest.

When The Toilet Won't Stop Running ... Check the tank float by first removing the lid and simply lifting the float. If it stops the water, bend the rod connected to the float down slightly. Also check for a leak in the float. Unscrew it from the rod and shake. Replace if there is water inside.

Tile Cracks ... Fix cracks around the bathtub by filling with tile cement. While it may not show, there could be water seepage into the ceiling of the floor below.

- Two lines of masking tape on either side of a crack to be caulked will prevent messes and leave a finished line after the caulking has dried.

Energy Savers

- Electrical appliances with heating elements such as stoves, dryers, and toasters, cost more to run than those with only motors. Be frugal and conserve energy.

- Invest in a 'clock thermostat'. There's no need to heat the entire house while you're at work, and the device will turn the furnace on at the time you desire.

- Going away for the weekend? Turn the hot water heater off and lower your thermostat to 60 degrees.

- Icicles may look very attractive hanging from your roof, but they're a sure sign of heat loss and pose a danger to those who walk under them. Have your attic insulated to keep the valuable heat inside.

- Shower instead of taking a bath. The average bath uses 20-30 gallons of water while the average shower uses only 10 gallons. Install a handshower in a showerless tub and save on water heating bills.

- A 25 watt fluorescent tube gives as much light as a 100 watt bulb.

- One 100 watt bulb gives off 50% more light than four 25 watt bulbs yet draws the same amount of current.

- Dusty bulbs can reduce the efficiency of your lighting fixture by as much as 75%.

○ Close the refrigerator door on a strip of paper. If you can remove it easily, you're wasting electricity and should replace the door stripping.

○ In order to operate at maximum efficiency, pilot lights on gas appliances should be regulated until the flame is blue with just a touch of yellow at the tip.

○ Insulate your basement ceiling and stop those annoying draughts from chilling your toes.

○ More hot water for less! Insulate your hot water tank and pipes.

○ A reflecting shield between radiators and walls prevents the wall from absorbing heat that you want circulating the room.

○ A soot-lined chimney is a fire hazard. Have it cleaned once a year and improve the efficiency of your fireplace.

○ Draw drapes or pull down window shades at dusk and leave them down until morning. The air pocket between the window and the drape forms a fair insulation layer.

○ Have your heating system fine tuned once a year. The service cost will be paid twice in saved fuel bills.

○ Dropping the temperature from 72 degrees to 68 degrees can save you as much as 15% on your heating bill. Drop it one degree each week to acclimatize yourself to the new temperature.

Miscellaneous

Loose Screws? ... Remove screw and fill hole with wood putty. Allow putty to harden overnight then replace screw.

○ If small screws in doorknobs and appliances keep coming unscrewed, try a touch of shellac on the head just before tightening.

○ Almost anything screws in clockwise and unscrews counterclockwise.

Drilling ... Whether in wood or metal, punch a small hole in the surface to prevent drill from skidding. Remember to have the object you are drilling firmly secured.

Ladders ... For every 4 feet up, your ladder should be at least 1 foot away from the wall.

○ Always keep your hips within the ladder rails.

- Extend your ladder at least two rungs higher than the place at which you are working.

Up On The Roof ... Clogged downspouts may fill with ice and burst. Try inserting wire mesh to prevent leaves and other debris from returning.

When You Can Smell Gas ... Never strike a match. Open windows immediately and call your local utility company.

Garage Clean Ups ... Remove oil drippings from concrete by placing several newspapers over the oil stain. Soak with water and allow to dry.

- Spread sand over the oil spill. Sweep up when sand has absorbed the oil.

- For stubborn oil stains on pavement, soak the area in mineral spirits and scrub vigorously. Soak up moisture with newspaper and allow to dry. Wash with a mixture of detergent, bleach and cold water.

Household Inventory ... It's always practical to keep track of household possessions and their value for insurance purposes. If this is a task you have long put off, try taking a walk through the house with a small cassette recorder. Describe the articles you see as you walk through each room and any particulars that may help identify it in the case of theft. Also note the value of the item. Keep the cassette in the car or at the office, and let's hope you never need it.

Identifying Keys ... Many hardware stores now carry various colored keys which will help identify the key you want in a hurry, but for existing keys, try marking with nail polish or acrylic paint in bright colors. Write down which keys are painted with what colors should you require reference.

- Another way to keep keys identified is to trace the outline of each key on a card and write down whether it belongs to the front or back door, etc. File cards in a safe place. Tape unused keys to cards with an appropriate description of where it fits.

Discourage Prowlers ... If you live in a house, leave a heavy dog chain hanging on the outside knob of the back door, or a large dog food dish close by. Most thieves will not go near a house that has evidence of a dog, let alone a very large dog.

Trouble Shooter

Check List . . . What to look for when one of your appliances acts up.

APPLIANCE	PROBLEM	POSSIBLE SOLUTION
Food mixers & blenders	Will not run.	Could be a dirty or defective speed control. Clean or replace.
	Lacks power on all settings	Could be a defective control switch. Try replacing the switch.
	Excessive noise and vibration.	The brushes may be worn or chipped. Replace.
Automatic clothes washer	Tub does not fill	The water hoses could be disconnected or blocked. Check for kinks or pinching in hoses.
	Tub does not drain	The drain hose may be blocked. Check for blockage and clean hose. (see All About Washing p. 70)
	No spin cycle	The drive belt may be loose or broken. Tighten the belt or replace if broken.
	Washer vibrates	Could be small or uneven load distribution. Rearrange garments and add a few towels if necessary.
Steam iron	No steam	Vents may be clogged with mineral deposits. Clean with a brush dipped in vinegar.
Coffee maker	Lukewarm water, but doesn't perk	Check thermostat and replace if defective — the circular unit located in the base.
Refrigerator	Interior not cold enough	Could be inadequate ventilation around the vents. Be sure refrigerator is well away from back wall so that air can circulate.

APPLIANCE	PROBLEM	POSSIBLE SOLUTION
Automatic dishwasher	Dishes not clean	The water may not be hot enough to thoroughly clean. Check domestic water temperature.
Electric clothes dryer	Does not start	The door interlock switch may be defective. Replace if necessary.
	Does not heat	May be defective heating element. Disassemble and check element, replace if necessary.
	Does not rotate	It may be that the drive belt is broken or the drum is sticking. Check for small articles that may cause drum to stick and/or replace drive belt if necessary.
Can opener	Slow running	The cutting edge may be dull or chipped. Sharpen or replace.
	Noisy	The gears may be defective. Try lubricating or replacing.
Portable fan	Fan erratic or slow	It may be the motor armature binding. Clean and lubricate the motor bearings.
	Fan vibrates	The blades may be unbalanced. Clean all accumulated dirt. If blades are bent, realign.
Vacuum cleaner	Little suction, motor is slow	The brushes and bearings may be worn. Replace brushes and try lubricating or replacing motor bearings.
	Little suction, motor is normal	The exhaust outlet may be blocked. Clean or replace filter.
Sewing machine	Slow and noisy	Lubrication may be required. Follow manufacturer's instructions.

APPLIANCE	PROBLEM	POSSIBLE SOLUTION
Waffle iron	Too much or too little heat	Check thermostat. Clean or replace if necessary.
	Waffles stick to grill	Grill not seasoned. Brush grill with cooking oil and heat for 30 minutes.
Toaster	Toast won't pop up	Bread may be caught in wires. Unplug toaster, remove bread, and shake out crumbs.
	Toast is too light or too dark	Linkage from color control to release mechanism may be broken or loose. Check that sliding parts are properly connected and replace if necessary.

THE MECHANIC

Preventive Maintenance

Reducing wear and tear on every part of your car not only saves costly repair charges but makes the car more energy efficient. Simple, regular and inexpensive care can save thousands of dollars and hours of inconvenience. Read on.

From The Ground Up: Tires... The air pressure in each tire should be checked four times a year to be certain it matches manufacturer's specifications. You'll save on both tire wear and gas consumption.

◦ If your car seems to shake or shimmy at certain speeds, the wheels may need to be balanced. Unbalanced or misaligned wheels can reduce tire life by one half. Have tires checked for balance every three months.

Changing Tires... You'll need a jack and preferably a relatively flat surface (to be remembered when you pull off to the side of the road). You'll also need a tool to remove the hubcap and a wrench to remove the nuts which hold the wheel on. Those are the same nuts originally installed at the factory using a powerful electronic tool. It's a good idea to loosen the nuts and then tighten them yourself before you encounter a flat tire.

1 Ply, 2 Ply, 3 Ply, 4 — What's The Difference?... The number of plys is simply the number of layers of material used to make the tire. Other numbers and letters indicate size and width on your tire. Read the car manufacturer's specifications to find out whay ply is suitable for your car.

Steel Belted Or Glass?... Tires are surrounded by a glass or steel belt covered with several plys, usually a synthetic material, and are warranted to last longer than regular tires. Some belted tires are advertised as year-round, but if you plan to drive in the snow, nothing beats two good snowtires for traction.

Flat Tires... Important! Always carry a spare. It's extremely dangerous, especially in cold weather, to be stuck on the road. A good hand pump can sometimes put enough air in your tire to get to a gas station. Better still are some commercial products which inflate your tire temporarily from a pressurized can.

○ Tires are tough but striking curbs, holes, rocks, or any hard object will severely shorten tire life. Check tires often for major defects.

○ All tires eventually wear out, but each tire on your car wears in a different spot. At least twice each year move each tire (including the spare) in a clockwise direction to the next wheel.

Brakes... The most important thing about a well-maintained, smoothly running automobile is that it is able to STOP as smoothly. At the first sound of squeaking brakes, have them checked.

Radiator... The temperature of burning gasoline (4,000°F) is hard on your engine. Keep it cool. If your car is standing in traffic the water in the radiator doesn't circulate around the engine. The car will overheat and stall. Simply allow the car to sit for 15 or 20 minutes with the engine disengaged.

○ Anti-freeze will prevent the water in your radiator from freezing and can be saved from season to season. Have the radiator flushed clean twice each year when changing to and from summer coolant.

○ The operating temperature of your engine is influenced by the environment. A winter thermostat should be installed in Autumn to keep the engine temperature consistent with outside conditions. A regular thermostat should be installed in the Spring.

Air Filters... Your car engine requires clean air to efficiently burn gasoline. Have the air filter checked every three months. Dust and grime can be washed from many filters with warm water and detergent, however filters should be replaced periodically.

Gasoline Filters ... Before gasoline is pumped from your gas tank into the engine, it travels through a filter, usually made of wire mesh, to remove suspended particles. Periodic inspection and cleaning will help to ensure a longer life for a host of moving engine parts.

Oil Filters ... Oil is continually circulating and recirculating through your engine. In the course of its travels the oil picks up small bits of carbon and other residue resulting from the combustion of gasoline. In order to act as an effective lubricant between moving metal surfaces, the residue must be removed from the oil by a filter. Eventually the filter will become clogged and must be replaced. Exactly when depends on how much driving you do and how efficiently your car burns gas. As a measure,if oil has changed in color from a light amber to black, it's a sign to change the oil and the filter.

Motor Oil ... Check your car's level regularly and while you're at it, check the color. Few things are more important to the proper maintenance of your engine than an adequate supply of a good quality oil. Many modern oils are advertised to last 40-50 thousand miles, but driving conditions, individual driving methods, and the condition of your car can make a tremendous difference in its longevity.

- ∘ If you have difficulty remembering when to change the oil in your car, or how long it has been since it was last lubricated etc., try clipping a small card to the underside of the sun visor and record all service details and dates on the card at the time of servicing. It's also a good idea to note mileage and gas consumption on the card.

Other Lubricants ... Older cars should have parts checked and lubricated more often than newer cars with self-lubricating systems.

Exterior — Locks ... If the lock sticks, try blowing powdered graphite into the keyhole. The graphite is usually sold in containers which facilitate such an application. Alternatively, rub your key with the point of a soft lead pencil. Oil in locks tends to collect grime and therefore impedes smooth operation.

- ∘ Frozen stiff! Never apply excessive force. Try inserting the key, then put a match to a twist of paper and hold close to the lock for 20 seconds. Be careful of that new paint finish.

- ∘ Or, try warming the key with a lighted match and reinserting in the frozen keyhole.

Rust... Remove small rust stains from bumpers and other chrome surfaces by scrubbing with fine steel wool soaked in kerosene.

○ Rust prevention techniques have improved dramatically in the last decade and a variety of treatments are now on the market. Most new cars have a rust perforation warranty or guarantee which means that you must have a hole caused by rust from the exterior to the interior before you can make a claim against the warranty.

○ One of the best rust prevention techniques is simply regular washing and waxing, especially during the winter months when salt builds up quickly on the exterior surface.

Windows... To remove pressure-sensitive stickers from the exterior of the car window, rub with nail polish remover or lighter fluid. Gently scrape with a razor blade.

○ For stubborn stickers, try saturating with salad oil before you begin scraping.

○ Plastic net bags (cooking onions are usually wrapped in them) will remove insects from the windshield without harming the glass. Some commercially available nylon pot scrubbers will do a good job too.

○ Baking soda on a damp rag will easily clean dust and grime from glass and chrome surfaces. Be sure to rinse with clean water and dry with a soft cloth.

○ Tired of scraping ice off your windshield? Store a box of fine grain salt in the trunk and rub on built up ice.

○ Replace windhsield wiper blades at least once a year. Driving with dirty or streaked windows is not only hard on your eyes and nerves, but is definitely dangerous.

○ Save yourself some time and trouble on cold winter mornings. If you are leaving your car outside at night, place floor mats on the front windshield and secure underneath the wipers. This will eliminate ice formation effectively.

○ Tar can be removed from the exterior by soaking the area in linseed oil. Allow a few minutes for the tar to soften then wipe with a clean cloth sprinkled with linseed oil.

○ Windshield washer is expensive. Try making your own with two quarts rubbing alcohol, 1 cup of water, and 1 teaspoon of detergent. Guaranteed not to freeze, even at -30°F.

Interior — Windows ... If you're tired of wiping the inside windows of your car while waiting for the defroster to take effect, try using a chalkboard eraser. It clears windows quickly and without streaking, and can be kept in the glove compartment.

Carpets ... Remove stubborn salt residue from carpeting by scrubbing with a mixture of one part vinegar to two parts water.

Smoldering Cigarettes ... Prevent this by placing an inch or two of sand or baking soda in the ashtray.

Starting the Car ... With new cars, follow the owner's manual exactly. For older cars, depress accelerator to the floor, release, then start the motor. Never let the starter run for more than a few seconds. Repeat starting procedure if necessary. If you can smell gasoline, it usually means the carburetor is flooded. Allow the car to sit for 10 or 15 minutes before trying to start again.

Starting Inventory ... You need a good battery, an efficient distributor which takes the charge from the battery and distributes it to the spark plugs, and you need clean spark plugs to ignite the gas effectively.

- In extremely cold weather, it may be necessary to wait until noon when the sun has warmed the car before trying to start it.

- Have your ignition timing checked in the Spring and Fall. If the spark plugs are sparking after the gasoline has entered the engine and not at exactly the same time, you will waste gas, lose power, and the car will not run smoothly.

- In extremely cold weather you may want to remove an old battery at night and reinstall it the next morning. But be careful; the fluid in the battery is corrosive and will turn your clothes to swiss cheese. Never smoke or bring a flame close to a battery or it may explode.

- Just in case — on very cold evenings and if you aren't 100% sure about the battery, try backing your car into the garage so that the battery is easily accessible for jumper cables.

Battery ... Heavy cables connect your car's starter to the battery posts. The battery post and the terminal on the cable may become badly corroded. Clean thoroughly with a solution of baking soda and water. To prevent corrosion, cover the terminals with petroleum jelly, making sure the connection between the battery post and the terminal is clean and secure.

- Most batteries do not require maintenance, but older batteries should be checked periodically. Each chamber in the battery has a plastic cap and distilled water should be added to keep the fluid level ½" above the top of the battery plates.

Distributor ... The distributor takes an electric charge from the battery and distributes it to each spark plug. It also contains moving parts which must be replaced periodically. Have it checked twice each year.

Spark Plugs ... Spark plugs receive an electric charge from the battery and send a spark across a gap only thousandths of an inch wide to ignite gas in the engine. This gap or space must be maintained exactly as specified in your owner's manual in order for your car to run efficiently. Have spark plugs checked twice a year and replaced if necessary.

Generator/Alternator ... Most older cars have a generator, while newer ones have an alternator. Both are responsible for producing all of the electricity your car needs for starting, radio, lighter, power windows etc. Both contain moving parts and should be checked twice a year.

Driving

Mountains ... The safest way to descend a steep hill is in low gear. Brakes, when used, should be applied intermittently to avoid burning out. If brakes feel low, stop and let them cool. Never coast with clutch disengaged or in neutral. On high mountain roads engines might only develop 50% of their expected horsepower and that means less power for accelerating and passing.

Cool Mornings ... Racing a cold engine greatly increases wear. Allow your car to warm-up before driving. Plan ahead during the winter months. Not only your engine will have a chance to warm up, but the passenger compartment will warm as well.

Speeding ... Keep speed moderate. High speeds consume more gas than slower speeds. Accelerate evenly and maintain a steady pace. Pedal pumping reduces efficient burning of gas.

Stopping ... After a long run, allow the engine to idle for a few minutes and cool gradually. Immediately switching the key off when the engine is very hot is hard on the mechanical parts, wastes gas, and tends to increase the build-up of waste residue in the cylinders.

- Avoid jumping starts and sudden stops. It's hard on gas, hard on the car, and hard on your nerves.

Driving With A Trailer ... Practice maneuvering the trailer in a vacant lot. Note that acceleration is more sluggish. You will need more room to pass and more room to stop. When turning, drive further into the intersection before starting the turn and avoid striking curbs. Don't forget when backing a trailer, the steering wheel is turned in the opposite direction from which you want the trailer to go.

Stuck In The Snow ... First try gently "rocking" the car. Don't race the engine and don't spin the rear wheels. Drive slowly forward, then stop. Drive slowly in reverse and stop. Repeat 10-12 times and if you're still stuck, proceed to Stage Two.

Stage Two — Stuck In The Snow ... If the rear wheels of your car are spinning in the snow or mud you must put something under them which will regain traction. Suggestions include salt, sand, ashes, boards, branches, floor mats, canvas. Some commercially available steel 'grids' which you carry in your trunk are useful if you regularly drive on difficult terrain.

Used Cars — Don't Get Stuck With A Lemon ... Don't be shy about taking a potential purchase to an independent mechanic for an objective opinion. The cost is minimal if you are planning to spend thousands on reliable transportation.

- Don't be shy about bargaining. If the dealer won't come down in price, he may have an extra pair of snow tires or that AM/FM radio that you really wanted.

NOTES:

Laundry Day Helpers

NOTES:

All About Washing

The Basics ... Never remove the manufacturer's washing instruction label from clothes or you may be in for trouble when it comes to laundering the garment. If it interferes with the wear by scratching or if it's visible, cut it out, but mark the instructions on a piece of paper and keep it in a recipe box above the washing machine.

- Before washing anything, sort laundry into convenient piles and wash separately: white cottons and linens; nylon and synthetics; silks and rayons; woolens; and non-color fast articles. Use very hot water for whites, and reduce water heat for synthetics, silks, woolens, and non-color fasts respectively.

- Remember to wash colored sheets and towels separately for the first few washes to remove any excess dye.

- Take a few minutes while sorting the wash to check for unusual stains or seams that have come apart. Mend seams before laundering to ensure that a small rip won't get caught in the dryer and ruin your garment completely.

- Check for grease stains before washing as well. Once a stain has been laundered it is impossible to remove.

- Washing machines need to be cleaned, too, from time to time. Pour a gallon of distilled vinegar into the washer and using warm water, let the machine run through a wash and rinse cycle. The vinegar will cut through built-up soap residue in hoses and leave your washer sparkling clean.

- One place you really can't save is laundry water. Using dirty water over again to do the next load may seem economical, but it will show in the color and feel of your wash. Always use clean soapy water, and rinse until the water is clear.

Delicate Laundry ... Those precious little garments can be washed gently and safely if you place them in a pillowcase and knot the open end before washing in your machine.

- Delicate washables should not be laundered using a harsh, all-purpose laundry detergent. Make your own 'weak' detergent by dissolving a cup of powdered soapflakes in a cup of warm water. Keep in a bottle for later use.

Laundry Powder Scoop ... Cut a plastic bleach jug in half. Use the top portion with its handle and cap secured, to scoop soap powder. Measure one cup of powder and mark the level with red nail polish for future accurate measuring.

Prevent Soap From Sticking ... Always dissolve soap powder detergents in warm or hot water before placing garments in the washer. Undissolved soap particles may lodge in corners of clothing, damaging the fabric.

Reducing Suds ... Salt sprinkled on suds will reduce the amount of lather and keep the machine from overflowing. But prevent this accident from happening by measuring detergent carefully.

Treating Hard Water ... Add washing soda to hard water BEFORE adding soapflakes to prevent a soap scum from forming.

- Washing soda turns hard water to soft water and reduces the amount of detergent required. If you are trying washing soda for the first time, go easy on the detergent.

- Soft water is much easier on fabrics than hard water. Repeated hard water use will weaken fabrics and sometimes turn whites grey. Use a commercial water softener or washing soda. As well as saving garments, it saves money because you need less detergent.

Mothers Beware! ... When laundering children's sleepwear, use a phosphate detergent. If you don't you may find that the flame retardents required by law on children's clothing will have lost their resistance. If you do use a non-phosphate detergent, make sure to add a cup of vinegar to the cold rinse water and allow garments to soak for ½ hour before starting the spin cycle.

Shape Preserver ... Keep your hand-washable sweaters in great shape by following this simple shape-preserver. Place the unwashed sweater on a clean, large sheet of paper. Place straight pins around the outline, affix to paper. After the sweater has been washed, work the shape around the pins and pin the garment to the paper. It will dry to exactly the right form.

Hosiery ... Hand-washing is the best and safest way to get the longest wear out of them. It takes about as much time at the end of the day as washing your hands. Keep a bar of soap or a container of 'weak' detergent in your bathroom cabinet just for hosiery, and watch how long they last!

- Nylon stockings that are dried in the dryer will create a lot of 'static cling'. Another reason to hand wash.

Washing Woolens ... Woolens are usually washable but take care. Use lukewarm water,never hot, with adequate sudsing. Don't leave it in the wash water longer than 15 minutes and rinse several times in clear cool water. Dry on a form or flat surface (see Shape Preserver for Sweaters).

○ For softer, fine woolen hand-washables, try adding a small amount of creme rinse to the final rinse water.

○ When your favorite woolen sweater is tossed in the wash by mistake, you may be able to salvage it. Try soaking in lukewarm water with a mild hair shampoo lather. If shrinkage is not severe, you may be able to reshape it.

○ Several drops of glycerin added to the final rinse water will soften woolens and make them less scratchy.

Cleaning the Uncleanables ... Even the dirtiest of clothes can be cleaned by adding 5 or 6 capfuls of household ammonia to wash water.

○ For whiter white socks, soak in hot water to which the juice of ½ lemon has been added.

Washing Non-Colorfast Garments ... Epsom salts will help prevent running and fading of non-colorfast items. Add 1 tsp. epsom salts per gallon of wash water for the first washing.

○ A teaspoon of ammonia added to wash water will also keep colors from running.

Old Fashioned Sugar Starch For Grandma's Doilies ... Boil 1 cup granulated sugar in 1/3 cup water for two minutes. Immerse doily until thoroughly soaked. Allow doily to drip dry, shaping as it dries.

Collar Rings ... Apply a paste of baking soda and vinegar. Work in with fingers around the shirt collar ring, then wash as usual.

○ Rub a small amount of hair shampoo along the collar 'ring' to loosen oils. If the ring doesn't fade while rubbing, try a small soft brush. Launder as usual.

○ An abrasive hand soap will work wonders as well.

○ Or try outlining the ring with chalk. The chalk will absorb oils, but may require several applications.

All About Drying

Solar Drying ... We've all heard about solar heating, but if you have a backyard and haven't considered drying your clothes on a line, think about it now. Clothes dryers use a lot of electricity to dry several loads. Line drying is a terrific way to conserve energy, and it really does leave clothes fresh-smelling and static-free.

- When line-drying trousers, hang them by the cuffs. The weight of the trousers will usually keep the legs wrinkle free, making pressing a simple job.

- When hanging a delicate dress or heavy coat outside on the line to dry, use two plastic coathangers hooked in the opposite direction. This will prevent the wind from blowing the garment off the line.

- Fine undergarments can usually be washed in the washing machine without damage but automatic dryers might turn the fabric grey. Keep a small clothesline in your laundry area or bathroom to hang dry lingerie.

Static Cling ... Instead of using costly sheet fabric softeners in the dryer, buy a budget liquid softener. Moisten an old face cloth and place in the dryer. Repeat for every load. Works just as well.

- A piece of wire will draw some of the static electricity if you run it along the garment.

Fluffy Feather Pillows ... Tumble in a cool dryer for about 10 minutes. For a really fresh lift, add a cloth dampened with liquid fabric softener to the dryer.

Pillowcases ... Pillowcases folded in pairs after laundering and pressing saves time when matching them later.

Did You Know ... A strong sun will weaken cotton fibres over a period of time, and intense cold will break fibres. So keep an eye on that clothesline, and bring clothes in as soon as they are dry.

- Cloth belts with synthetic backing should not be sent to the cleaners. Solvents used in cleaning will weaken the backing and leave the belt limp.

'Lintless' Laundry ... Try adding ½ cup of white vinegar to the final rinse.

- Dampen a clothes brush and brush clothes downward in even strokes.

- Check dryer filters often for signs that may indicate a bit of repair work is needed. Damp lint on the filter may mean a clogged vent. Check outside vents periodically.

- Nylon netting will catch lint if placed in your dryer along with the regular load.

Removing The Fuzz ... Sweaters that have pilled can be restored by gently shaving the surface with a clean razor.

All About Ironing

Efficient Ironing Ideas ... 'Insulate' your ironing board with foil. The foil will reflect heat back to the underside of the item you're pressing.

- It makes sense to follow a few simple rules to avoid having to re-press sleeves and collars. First press all parts of the garment that can hang from sides of the ironing board, such as sleeves, cuffs and belts. Then iron the main body of the garment without disturbing those already-pressed pieces. Make sure you iron fabrics until completely dry.

- Ironing pre-dampened garments is much easier if they are folded lightly after sprinkling. Tight folding creates extra wrinkles and work.

- Here's a great idea for ironing rough, dry garments in a hurry. Sprinkle with lukewarm water, roll tightly and place in a plain paper bag. While the iron is heating, place the bag in a warm oven. By the time the iron is hot, the garment will have warmed and will be thoroughly damp.

- To prevent mildew, never leave dampened clothes for too long before ironing. Keeping them in the refrigerator will prevent mildew, but the best solution is to schedule to iron later in the day.

Smoother Collars ... When pressing shirt collars, work from the corners into the back of the collar to prevent wrinkling along the front edges of the collar.

Glazed Chintz ... Glazed chintz should be ironed on the right side in order to bring out the lustre of the fabric.

Shoulder Pads ... Shoulder pads are back in fashion, but when laundering new styles follow the old-fashioned rules: remove pads before laundering if at all possible. If not, make sure they are completely dry before ironing sleeves to avoid ugly rings.

Ironing Wool Blends ... Blended fabrics of wool and rayon should be ironed as if 100% wool. Steam press using a damp cloth.

Two 'Bright' Ideas ... A quick way to press ribbons is to run the ribbon over a clean warm light bulb. Saves getting the iron and ironing board out.

- When you've forgotten the travel iron, a warm light bulb will help get light creases out of cottons and woolens. Dust and wipe bulb, turn on and allow to warm and turn off before passing the creased area over the bulb.

Tablecloths That Last... It's a good idea to change the way you fold tablecloths from time to time. Continued pressing and folding will weaken the material along the crease lines.

Tucks & Pleats... There really is a trick to ironing tucks so they'll be neat and flat. Make sure you iron slowly so that material can be thoroughly dried. If they are still somewhat damp, tucks will wrinkle soon after ironing. Press vertical tucks horizontally, pulling the material taut as you iron. Horizontal tucks should be pressed by starting at the top and working slowly to the bottom.

Embroidery Magic... Place a turkish towel on the ironing board and iron embroidery work face down on the towel. This will guarantee a smooth finish, even in the tiniest of spaces.

Restoring Velvet... Restore velvet garments by brushing thoroughly with a soft brush in the direction of the nap. Then steam it on the wrong side and hang to dry.

Softening Chamois... Soak in a bucket of warm water to which a capful of olive oil has been added.

Cleaning Your Iron... Remove brown spots by rubbing with fine steel wool dipped in warm vinegar.

- Polish with toothpaste! That's right. Apply and allow to dry. Buff with a soft cloth.

- Remove deposits from the steam system by filling with equal parts vinegar and water. Allow the iron to steam for 2 or 3 minutes. Let it cool for an hour. Rinse well.

On Removing Stains

Home Made Spot Remover... Make your own commercial spot remover. Simply add 1 part rubbing alcohol to 2 parts water. Simple as that!

Suede... Removing a stubbord stain on suede can be very simple. If ordinary brushing doesn't do the trick, try rubbing the spot lightly with an emery board, then steam over a boiling kettle. Just like new.

Blood Stains On Clothing... Blood stains can be removed by applying a paste of meat tenderizing crystals and cold water. Allow ½ to ¾ hour to set. Rinse in cool water.

Wax Removal ... Crayon marks and candle wax can be easily removed from clothing. Cut two pieces of brown paper to cover both sides of the stained area and press with a warm iron. The wax should melt and stick to the paper.

Gum Removal ... To get rid of chewing gum, even from hair, put the white of an egg on it and leave for a few minutes. Work the gum out.

Double Knits ... Try sprinkling club soda over grease stains on double knits. It works!

Ballpoint Pen Ink ... Rubbing alcohol dabbed on the stained area may lift the ink right out. It's worth a try.

- Try using hair spray to remove ballpoint ink stains.

- Remove ink stains on colored garments by soaking the garment in milk.

- Remove ink stains on white fabrics by rubbing the area with a mixture of lemon juice and salt. If possible, hang to dry in a sunny place.

Rust Stains ... Remove rust from clothing or fabrics by applying lemon juice and salt. Hang outside in the sun to dry.

- Cover the area with cream of tartar. Roll tightly and soak in a bucket of hot water, then launder as usual.

Perspiration Stains ... Place garment in a bucket of warm water with 1 cup vinegar added. Soak for an hour or so before laundering.

Tar ... Rub the area with kerosene before laundering, but to be sure to check for color fastness before applying kerosene.

Scorch Stains ... Dampen a piece of cloth with a weak solution of peroxide and press over scorched area.

Removing Wine Stains ... Sprinkle immediately with salt to absorb as much of the wine as possible. Rinse in cold water rubbing lightly. Allow to dry. Check if any stain remains and repeat if necessary before laundering.

More Clothing Hints ... See Hints For Your Wardrobe
pgs. 108, 109, 110.

NOTES:

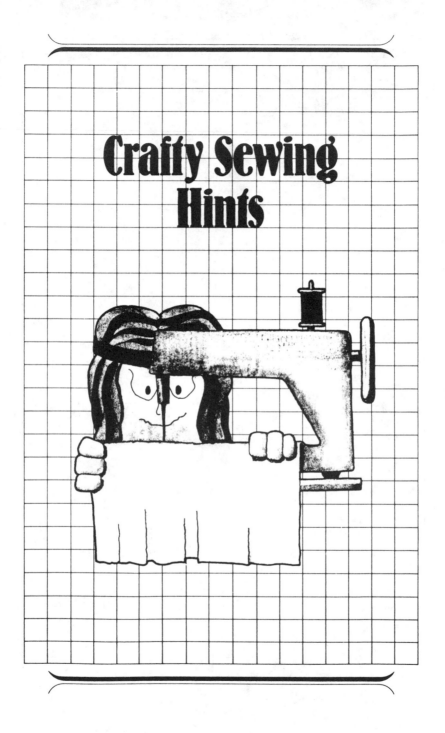

Crafty Sewing Hints

NOTES:

TIPS TO EASE THOSE SEWING BLUES

Time Savers... Being organized is the first key to saving time when sewing. Find a small area in your home where you can set up your machine and leave it. Convert an unused closet into a sewing room, or screen off a small corner of a large room. Being able to leave your sewing without having to pack up saves valuable time.

○ When buying fabric for a new outfit, buy everything you'll need to complete the project all at once and avoid trips to the store later.

○ Try leaving your hand-sewing in a decorative basket by the telephone or your favorite chair. You can have a chat with friends or watch television and get a few hems and buttons done as well.

○ You must press garment pieces as you go, but why not collect a few pieces and press at one time. Remember though, never sew across a seam unless it has first been pressed.

○ If you are interrupted just as you're ready to press garment pieces, set them aside and iron along with your regular ironing. When you next have some time to sew, your pieces will be ready.

○ Do all top-stitching at one time to avoid having to rethread your machine.

○ Make a simple sewing apron with pockets to wear when sewing or mending. Tape a cloth tape measure to the hem for quick rule, and store your mending equipment in the pockets.

Money Saver... A lot of money can be saved by using your local library as a source for knitting and crochet patterns. Most libraries have a good selection of instruction books, as well as many patterns. Write out the patterns you particularly like and note the publication and page before returning the book to the library.

Quick And Easy Pattern Cutting... Instead of pinning your pattern to fabric, tape it. It's much easier and keeps the pattern from tearing. When cutting out, the tape is easily cut and removed from the fabric.

○ Cut ¼" snips into seams instead of notches.

○ Cut straight seams on the selvage and eliminate time consuming seam finishing.

- When planning to sew more than one garment save time by cutting the pieces all at once.

Long Lasting Patterns ... A pattern sprayed with sizing before pressing will last longer.

- If you really love that pattern and plan to use it often, make all the necessary adjustments and cut it out on a heavier paper (kraft parcel wrapping paper is ideal). Punch a hole in a corner of each pattern piece and store your new pattern on a coat hanger. Remember to write down any instructions you need on one of the pieces, or clip the manufacturer's instruction sheet to a large piece.

Tailor's 'Soap' ... When a bar of soap is down to a thin piece, allow it to dry and use it in place of tailor's chalk to mark darts, pleats, hems etc. The mark is easily erased with a light brush of the finger.

Trick Darning ... Cut a small piece of paper and place it on the underside of the hole about to be darned. Stitch back and forth on your machine until the entire hole has vanished. Then launder. The water will soften and dissolve the paper leaving a very neat and quick mending job.

Darning Gloves ... When darning a very small rounded area such as the tip of a glove finger, drop one of the children's marbles into the finger and you'll have a perfect darning egg.

Darning Socks ... Use the lighted end of a flashlight as a darning egg when mending dark colored socks. Turn it on, and see every stitch!

- Place a piece of netting over the area to be darned and using the net as a guide, darn through it.

- Place a moth ball in the centre of woolen yarn as you're winding to keep the moths away.

Knotless Thread ... After threading the needle, be sure to knot the end that was cut closest to the spool to help eliminate tangles.

No More Knotting ... Eliminate the need to knot thread ends of seams by back stitching at the beginning and end of each piece.

- Never knot ends when thread basting. One pull will then remove the entire length of thread.

- Use cellophane tape to keep spooled thread from unravelling.

Pins & Needles ... A bit of hairspray or starch rubbed on the end of thread before threading through the needle will make the task much easier.

- Sharpen your machine needle by running it through a piece of sandpaper several times.

- Straight pins on the floor? Keep a small magnet handy for quick pick-ups.

- Wrap a piece of flannel around the main arm of your machine. When sewing, pins can be removed and stuck into the flannel without stopping.

Dual Purpose Pin Cushion ... Sewing machine needles are easily kept in a small scented soap bar. They'll sew more smoothly when used and will add a nice fragrance to your working area.

Buttons & Buttonholes ... Buttons will stay on longer if you sew through only two holes at a time. Break the thread and knot before starting on the next pair of holes.

- Dab a bit of clear nail polish on the centre of each sewn button to help prevent threads from breaking. If you want extra strength, try sewing buttons with dental floss.

- When making buttonholes, prevent frayed centres by painting the buttonhole mark with clear nail polish. After it has dried, snip with a razor blade.

Zippers That Won't Zip ... Sticky zippers come unstuck when sprayed heavily with starch or when they are rubbed with a candle.

Warehousing Fabric ... Storing material for projects you plan to do is a great idea as long as you remember for which pattern you bought the fabric. Pin a slip of paper to the folded fabric noting its measurements and the pattern number you plan to make.

- If you want to take advantage of fabric sales, keep a list in your wallet with the various yardages required for your favorite patterns.

Scissors ... Sandpaper puts the fine sharp edge back on your scissors. Simply snip through a piece of sandpaper several times.

Portable Needle & Thread Case ... Old lipstick tubes can be used to store emergency needles and thread. Clean out the tube thoroughly using an old mascara brush and soap. Rinse and dry. Place a small amount of cotton in the bottom of the tube to serve as a lining. Store a threaded needle and several lengths of white, black, blue or brown thread in the tube and carry in your cosmetic bag.

Matchbook Uses... Push several pins into match stick stubs on the inside cover and wind thread around the closed matchbook for a travelling sewing kit.

○ Use the cover to hold razor blades when ripping seams or removing button threads.

Cheap Storage Containers... Use old adhesive tape containers to wind and store measuring tapes, bias tape, hem binding, and mending wool.

Recycling... Towels have many uses long after they are ready to be discarded. Try sewing three or four together for a family beach blanket, or make beach pillows out of old facecloths stuffed with shredded nylons or discarded material.

Cast Iron Handle Holders... Cut an old pot holder in half. Using the half with the little loop for hanging, sew a seam to join two edges forming a tube. Slip over the handle of your cast iron pan, and double the life of that old pot holder!

Ski Pants... Make cross-country ski pants from a pair of old corduroy pants. Cut the legs off below the knee and sew on wide knit sleeve cuffs to finish. Hemming with elastic also works well. Spray with fabric protector.

Quilts... Make a patchwork quilt by saving your children's clothing and cutting pieces to fit your pattern. The little ones will love it.

○ Use pinking shears to cut squares out of an old quilted crib cover and use the pieces as pot holders.

Yarn That Won't Tangle... Use handy food storage baggies for keeping wool clean and tangle free. Place skein of wool in bag, punch a hole in the bag and thread a strand of yarn through. Seal with an elastic band.

Net Curtains... Use clear nail polish to rejoin tears in net curtains. You may have to repeat the procedure after every washing.

Great Pin Ups... Place a 2' x 2' piece of pegboard on the wall over your cutting table or sewing machine. Insert a screw into each hole in the board to store spools of thread.

○ A few squares of adhesive cork placed on the wall over your machine is a handy place to pin up pattern instructions.

Lovers' mittens ... For brisk winter walks with someone you love, try making a pair of lovers' mittens. Simply use an old pair of mitts, or buy an inexpensive woolen pair at a thrift store (usually available for under $2). Cut the thumbs away, and working from the inside, stitch openings of both mittens together. Holding hands in cold weather — with a personal touch.

NOTES:

Children's Corner

NOTES:

TIPS FOR TOTS

Bottled And Certified Hints ... When cleaning bottles in your sterilizer, place some marbles in it. The marbles will gather all the corrosion.

○ To free baby bottles from mineral deposits, add lemon juice to the water when boiling the bottles.

○ Make a baby bottle holder from six-pack cardboard soft drink containers. Very convenient when travelling or at home.

○ Wrap aluminum foil around glass bottles to keep them warm while baby's feeding.

Rub A Dub Dub, Baby And The Tub ... Put small pieces of soap into a cotton sock and tie the end. Perfect for small hands and it won't slip away!

○ Use your infant seat for bathing baby in the tub. Remove the pad, buckle the strap and put a folded towel in the seat. Place baby in the seat and into the water. Keep both hands free!

○ Rub cold cream over the eyelids and around the eyes of children before shampooing their hair to keep the soap out.

Bedtime Stories ... When baby is up for his night feedings turn a heating pad on warm and place it on his mattress. Remove the heating pad before returning the baby to his warm bed. He will settle down much more quickly.

Cribs To Beds ... Your child is graduating from his crib to a bed. Put his crib mattress on the floor next to his bed. If your child accidentally falls out he will not be hurt.

Toytown ... Small children have less trouble holding on to the strings of toys if you hang a large button or bead on the end of them.

Emergency Sand Shovel & Pail ... Cut a clean plastic bleach jug half. Give your child the half with the handle to use as a shovel and the bottom half as a pail.

Making Paste ... Dissolve 2 tbls. of laundry starch in a little cold water and add a cup of boiling water. Boil until thick. It won't gum up children's fingers but if any should get on their clothes, let it dry and brush off.

Preserving Artwork For Posterity ... Save your child's artwork. Apply a coating of hairspray to the drawing. This keeps colors from fading or wearing.

Bobbles, Bangles & Beads ... Keep children amused for hours by giving them things like macaroni, beads, spools, buttons, yarn and other odds and ends you may have around. These things can be strung to make necklaces or bracelets or glued on paper plates to make an interesting collage.

Buttering Up Your Children ... You and your child can make homemade butter easily. Pour a pint of whipping cream into a quart size covered jar and shake until the cream thickens. Add a little salt to make salted butter.

Messing Around ... Cut old shirts off at the sleeves and use as coveralls when your child is eating or painting.

Play Dough ... Make your own.
  4 cups flour
  ½ cup salt
  4 tsp. alum
  2-2 ½ cups boiling water
  food coloring

  Mix boiling water and food coloring. Then add the other three ingredients and mix well. Let cool. Keep in your refrigerator uncovered for one day, then cover.

Finger Paint ... An old-fashioned recipe.
  ½ cup powdered laundry starch
  ¾ cup cold water
  1 pkg. gelatin
  ¼ cup cold water
  2 cups hot water
  ½ cup powdered detergent
  food coloring

  Mix first two ingredients and in a separate container, allow gelatin to soak in the ¼ cup of cold water. Add hot water to the starch mixture and boil until the solution is clear, stirring constantly. Remove from heat and stir in gelatin mixture and soap until fully dissolved and thickened. Pour 1 cup into each of three containers (old coffee tins with plastic lids are great) and add food coloring to each container.

Stuffed Animal Farm ... Rub dry cornstarch into the toy. Let it stand briefly and then brush the cornstarch off.

  ○ For unwashable stuffed toys that need cleaning try this. Mix 1 tablespoon of liquid detergent with ½ cup of liquid fabric softener in a quart of warm water. Brush this on the toys (use an old, soft toothbrush), but do not saturate the article, and rub them with a clean soft towel. When dry they will be fresh, clean and soft.

Nursery Ideas — Room For Improvement ... Replace ordinary dresser knobs with small wooden alphabet blocks or wooden animal toys. Remove knobs and glue on new drawer pulls with epoxy.

  ○ Brighten up your child's room by covering an entire wall with bright colored felt or burlap. Your child can 'tape-up' his favorite paintings and pictures without damaging the fabric.

Picture Perfect ... If you are running out of space to hang your child's drawings and paintings try this:
Hang a fishnet in your child's room and use colored clothespegs to hang the pictures on the fishnet!

Travelling The Tidy Way ... Hang a shoe bag over the back seat of the car and store all your travelling knick knacks and children's toys.

  ○ When your youngster gets fidgety during long distance driving, have a 'beat the car race'. Pull over to a seldom used side road and have junior run along side the car, trying to get ahead of it. He'll soon wear off that extra energy while having fun at the same time.

  ○ Use small paper plates to slip onto popsicle and ice cream sticks and avoid messy drips.

Clothes Closet ... Soda water will remove the odor caused from baby's spit-ups. Gently rub the area with a cloth dampened with soda water.

Shoe Things ... Avoid falls in new shoes. Sand or scratch the soles lightly on pavement 2 or 3 times.

  ○ Before polishing, rub shoes with rubbing alcohol.

  ○ Or rub shoes with a raw potato before polishing and polish with an old nylon stocking.

  ○ After polishing allow to dry thoroughly and buff with waxed paper.

  ○ Teach your child to put his shoes on. Mark or tape the right shoe only. He'll be able to identify it quickly.

Safety Hints ... Tie a small bell to your door. When your child tries to sneak outside you will hear the bell ring.

- ○ Teach your child that red means danger. Use red fingernail polish to paint harmful bottle caps.

- ○ To avoid toddlers walking into sliding glass doors, place a piece of colored tape on the glass at eye level. This will alert him when the door is closed.

Grandma's Remedies

Ouches!... Saturate a piece of cotton with baby oil and rub over adhesive tape on your child's skin. No ouch!

Toothaches... Apply clove oil or a whole clove against the aching tooth to relieve pain.

Chapped Lips Or Hands... Apply glycerin and lemon juice in equal amounts. Smooth glycerin on chapped hands and leave overnight.

Nausea... Drink a cup of warm water with 20 drops of essence of peppermint. Sweeten if you must.

Coughs... Boil a whole lemon and extract the juice. Add 1 oz. glycerin and 1 cup honey. Stir. Administer 1 teaspoon three times a day.

Sore Throat... Gargle with salt water.

- ○ Drink fresh pineapple juice or a teaspoon of cider vinegar in a glass of water.

Headache... Rotate head to relieve tense neck muscles. Inhale fumes from boiled apple cider vinegar. Apply a cold towel to eyes and rest quietly for a few minutes.

Splinter... Apply rubbing alcohol to area and remove with eyebrow pluckers. If imbedded totally, sterilize a needle with alcohol and work splinter out from the bottom. If necessary, numb the area with an ice cube first.

- ○ To remove splinters more easily soak the injured area in olive oil for a few minutes.

Bee Stings... Apply a mud paste or paste of baking soda and water. Dab with lemon juice.

- ○ Dab on cider vinegar to relieve itch.

Minor Cuts... Sterilize and apply castor oil to aid healing process.

NOTES:

NOTES:

Gardening
with a Green Thumb

NOTES:

PLANTS & FLOWERS

Ideas For Your Soil Enjoyment

A 'Clover' Idea ... Place a clove of garlic in plant soil to eliminate bugs. The garlic keeps the nasty bugs away, and will also grow along with your plant.

- Place several matches into soil so that the sulphur tip is covered. This will definitely ward off worms.

My Plant Is Bugged! ... Wash leaves with a very mild detergent solution to remove many common bugs.

Save Your Soot ... It makes excellent fertilizer for your garden and potted plants.

Homemade Fertilizer ... A crystalline compound called "Urea" is available at drug stores and makes an inexpensive fertilizer. One teaspoon to a gallon of water.

Fern Goodness Sake ... Try this homemade fertilizer on your ferns. Four raw oysters finely chopped and worked into the soil. What a treat!

Falling Ferns ... Spruce up an ailing fern by substituting diluted tea instead of its normal water solution. This procedure should only be repeated once each month until the fern returns to normal.

Get Crackin' ... Rejuvenate ailing plants by watering with a mixture of egg shells and water. Allow shells to sit in water for 24 hours prior to watering plants, but be sure not to leave it any longer.

Branching Out To Leaves And Stems

Dust Is A Nasty Word ... And can filter as much as 50% of the sunlight that your plant needs to be healthy. Use a feather duster for quick, gentle cleaning.

Leaves Leaves Shining ... Use a few drops of glycerin on a soft cloth to put a sheen on plant leaves.

Withering Foliage ... Give your plant a boost by adding a tablespoon of castor oil mixed with its regular water.

Stem Gems ... Chopsticks make terrific splints for leaning stems.

- A popsicle stick taped to a weak or broken stem might save that little plant.

The Watering Hole

What's On Tap... If you use tap water, let it stand in a bucket for a few days before watering your plants. This will allow water to warm to room temperature and most of the harmful chemicals will settle in the bottom of the bucket.

○ The best water for plants is rainwater. It's naturally the right temperature and does not contain chlorine. Keep a 'rainbarrel' outside in summer and treat your plants to nature's bounty. In winter, collect a bucket of clean snow and let it melt.

Plant Sitters... They're harder to find than a good babysitter. If you're going away for a week and want to treat your plants kindly, try this hint: Use a length of cloth cording long enough to bury several inches into the soil and to reach a large container of water, set slightly above the plant. This is particularly useful for large plants that are difficult to move.

○ For smaller plants, try constructing a miniature greenhouse by first watering the plant and then covering with a plastic bag. Secure at one end with an elastic band or twist tie and move away from direct sunlight.

○ Or, fill the bathtub with several inches of water (make sure the faucet isn't left dripping). Set plants on bricks inside the tub but don't sit directly in water. Check to be sure that all pots have drainage holes, and have a carefree vacation!

○ Just one more...A washable blanket placed in the tub with an inch or two of water will hold enough moisture to keep plants from drying out. Sit plants directly on top of the blanket.

Oops I Forgot To Water The Plants... If the soil has crusted, most of the water you pour will run directly out of the pot. This calls for immediate attention. Loosen the soil as much as possible with a fork without damaging the roots. Work some peat moss or vermiculite into the top layers of soil, and finally give the plant a good sink soaking.

Oh, Those Thirsty Plants... Overwatering is as dangerous as underwatering and depending on the humidity and placement of a plant, it may require a different watering schedule than its offshoot across the room. As a general rule of thumb, sink your finger into the soil to test for moisture. If it feels dry, then water; if not, pass by and test again in a few days.

Transplanting And Other Environmental Concerns

New Plants... Keep newly purchased plants, or plants you bring in from the garden, away from the rest of your collection until you are sure the new addition is healthy and bug-free.

Potting Materials ... Collect materials such as stones, walnut shells, and fruit pits. Place in the bottom of each pot to allow adequate drainage.

- Don't throw out that broken clay pot. Hammer it several times and use the pieces to provide drainage when repotting.

When To Transplant ... Transplant when root-bound or when growth has stopped, but never to a pot more than 2" larger than the present container.

When Sunlight Hurts ... Leave a newly transplanted plant out of direct sunlight for a few days to allow roots to grow again. Snip away tiny budding leaves to promote root growth.

- Even if you are just moving the plant from one place in the house to another, the shock may give it a temporary set-back. So take care when rearranging.

Removing The Rootball From The Pot ... Never pull a plant out by the stem. Tap several times on the bottom of the pot. Using a spoon, gently loosen surrounding soil and lift the entire root and stem with one motion. Shake gently and place in the new container.

Pots, Pans And New Plant Ideas

Hawaiian Delight ... An exotic plant will grow from the top of a pineapple planted in a jar of water.

Vine Line ... Sweet potatoes planted in sandy soil will produce an attractive hanging vine with dark green leaves.

Pots, Pans And Other Plantholders ... Place some miniature geraniums in an old basket lined with aluminum foil.

- Save the plastic base of your solid air freshener. Clean thoroughly and place a miniature african violet in it.

- An old wooden salad bowl makes an interesting container for your cactus garden. Place several layers of foil in the bottom and fill with 2" of coarse gravel. Add a sandy mixture and arrange your desert garden.

- An unused copper teapot makes a lovely container for "baby tears". Line the inside of the teapot with a good layer of petroleum jelly and place the pot of little darlings inside. They'll grow to cover the entire pot.

- Do the same with a chipped or lidless fancy sugar bowl. But this time place a few clay pieces on the bottom and fill with soil. Now you'll have a matching centrepiece for your table settings.

- Glue five fancy bathroom tiles together with epoxy — one for the bottom and four for the sides to make an attractive plantholder for the kitchen or bathroom.

- Make a decorative hanging planter by weaving ribbon through the top slots of several plastic strawberry containers placed inside one another. Tie colored cord to each corner and knot at the top.

Cut Flowers

Beautiful Bouquets . . . If the stems are dark tipped snip half an inch and place in deep cool water.

- Always remove leaves below the waterline to avoid contaminating the water.

- Change water daily to help flowers last longer.

- When cutting stems, use a sharp knife or scissors and cut while holding under cold water. This prevents air from forming tiny pockets in the lower stem.

- Splice the ends of large stems to allow greatest absorbtion of water.

- Add a spoon of sugar plus a few drops of lemon juice to vase water. This helps keep flowers fresher and avoids unpleasant odors.

- Wilted flowers will perk up if you place the stems in hot water for 20 minutes. Replace in regular vase water.

- Place a few layers of colorful stones in bottom of a vase if the flower stems are too short.

- To make stems longer, fit stem into plastic straw.

- To keep long stemmed flowers upright in the vase place thin pieces of tape across the mouth of the vase to form a criss-cross pattern.

- Spray cut flowers with hairspray the day before they wilt to enjoy several extra days of pleasure from them and to prevent petals from dropping off. Spray from beneath the vase in an upward direction.

Drying Flowers... Prepare a mixture of 30% borax and 70% white
cornmeal. Cover flowers entirely with mixture and leave for
several weeks.

VEGETABLE GARDENING

Tips For The Best Crop In Town

Choosing The Right Location... The best of sites receive sun all
day, but at least six hours of midday sun is required.

- Be careful not to plant too close to buildings or trees that cast
  shade. Tree roots also soak up essential nutrients.

- Avoid low-lying areas that collect water and promote root rot.

Planning The Garden... Perennials such as rhubarb and
asparagus should be kept at the outer edge of the garden or in
a separate area to avoid damage when plowing the rest of
the garden.

- Rows should run north to south so plants won't shade each
  other. Keep corn at the north end or separately to avoid
  shading smaller crops.

- Instead of planting lettuce all at once, plan several small
  plantings so you'll have it all summer instead of more than you
  can use all at once.

- Keep a diagram and notebook for your garden, jotting down
  planting dates and maturity dates. You'll also want to keep
  track of ideas you have for next year's garden.

Getting Ready... Before digging the soil, test for dampness. Soil
should be fairly dry and should crumble when rubbed
between your fingers.

- Lift soil in chunks, turn and shatter with spade or pitchfork.

- Follow manufacturer's instructions on fertilizers, remembering
  less is better.

- After fertilizing, rake surface smooth.

Seeding Indoors... Save egg cartons, milk cartons, and shallow
aluminum trays for starting seeds.

- Use a good planting medium and fill containers. Vermiculite
  and equal amount of milled sphagnum moss is ideal.
  Dampen mixture.

- Scatter seeds over surface and press firmly into soil. Cover with ⅛ to ¼" potting soil.

- Cover containers with damp newspaper or dark green plastic and store in a warm damp place. Check daily.

- The secret of successful indoor seeding is warmth (70-80°F) and dampness.

- Once seeds have sprouted, remove plastic or paper covering and place in an area with 12 hours of light a day, preferably a bright light. If you haven't a spot that sunny, ordinary fluorescent lighting will do as long as the seedlings are kept about 3" from the light. (A fluorescent desk lamp has a double se here).

- Temperature can be lowered to 55-60°F once seeds have reached this stage. Water when soil surface is dry to the touch.

- Allow second pair of leaves to form before transplanting to the garden. Thin seedlings if necessary to allow room for growth.

Transplanting Seedlings ... Transplanting will help the growth of strong roots. Use a mixture of equal parts potting soil, sphagnum moss and perlite.

- Gently uproot by lifting with a spoon, taking care not to disturb roots or surrounding soil too dramatically.

- Place in the new mixture about 3" apart forming a small hole in soil first. Pour water in the hole, and fill remainder of hole with mixture, making sure roots are firmly planted. Allow to rest in shade several hours.

- Keep a close check on seedlings, making sure there is sufficient air circulation (no crowding please) and sun- light. Check soil dampness daily and water when it feels dry to touch. Indoor plant fertilizer can be added to watering solution one week after transplanting or when second pair of leaves are well developed.

Planting Your Garden ... Cut intersecting lines in plant containers using a sharp knife. Do not remove from container, simply sever joining roots inpreparation for outdoors. Allow two weeks before transferring to garden for strong rootballs to form. Allow containers to sit outside for several hours a day in part shade to prepare for the outdoors. Reduce watering for the week preceding planting.

- Dig small holes in garden soil and remove seedling from container. Place in hole and fill with loose soil. Water and press firmly in place.

○ Make sure stem is planted to second pair of leaves. If stakes will be required later, drive them in now in order to avoid damaging a well formed root later on.

○ If strong winds or rain occurs within a few days of planting outdoors, protect seedlings by covering with inverted buckets or containers.

NOTES:

and finally
...Just for You

NOTES:

TIPS TO BEAUTIFY YOU

Masks & Scrubs To Make At Home

A Face "Sauna" ... Enjoy a gentle facial steaming to cleanse pores and bring color to your cheeks. In a saucepan, bring water to a boil. Add lemon juice and mint leaves. Remove saucepan from the heat and place on the counter. Cover your head with a towel and allow towel to drape over the steaming pot. Steam for five minutes, and splash face with cool mineral water. Pat dry.

Oatmeal Scrub ... This treatment acts as great slougher and helps remove blackheads and other skin impurities. Mix together ¼ cup coarse oatmeal, 1 tsp. honey, and enough buttermilk to make a paste. Apply to the face and neck, making sure not to cover the eye area. Using fingertips, massage gently in a circular motion. Allow to dry and rinse with cool, refreshing water. Your skin will feel as smooth as a baby's bottom.

Oatmeal Mask ... Mix 1 tblsp. oatmeal with the white of an egg. Apply to face and allow to dry. If you have very dry skin, apply some mayonnaise after the mask, and rinse with warm water. If skin is oily, smooth on some plain yoghurt after cleansing.

Avocado & Egg White Mask (For Normal Skin) ... Make a paste of 1 medium avocado mashed, ½ tsp. lemon juice and the white of one egg that has been beaten until frothy. Apply to skin and allow to dry. Rinse with cool water.

Egg Yolk & Olive Oil Mask (For Dry Skin) ... Mix together the yolk of one egg, slightly beaten, & 2 tsp. of olive oil added in drops to the egg. Apply this heavy cream and allow to dry. Rinse with cool water.

Strawberry Mask (For Oily Skin) ... Add ½ cup mashed strawberries and 1 tsp. of lemon juice to form a paste. Apply and allow to dry, then rinse with cool water. You can substitute cucumber or tomato puree for strawberries and enjoy the same refreshing result.

Fuller's Earth ... Make a smooth paste using water and Fuller's Earth. Apply and leave on for several minutes. Rinse with cool water to remove.

Apricot Delight ... Before going to bed, put 6 dried apricots in water to soak. The following morning puree apricots in a blender. Apply to face and leave on for 5 minutes. Remove with tepid water.

Toners & Astringents

Witch Hazel... A terrific and inexpensive toner. Buy it at your local drug store and dab it on with a cotton ball. Refreshing!

PH-Balanced Toner... The juice of one lemon combined with a quart of mineral water makes an excellent skin toner or astringent. Dab on after cleansing for a refreshing lift.

Cucumber Astringent... Blend a few pieces of cucumber and strain through a small tea strainer to remove pulp. Mix cucumber juice with several drops of honey and stir. Refrigerate in a covered small bottle. Dab on with cotton balls after cleansing for a fresh, tingly toner. The mixture will keep for several days and is well worth the effort to make it.

Moisturizers

The Perfect Moisturizer... Water is the best moisturizer for skin, but mineral water is even more vitalizing. Wash out an unused small spray bottle and keep on your dresser top for instant freshness. After spraying your face lightly, rub in a dab of petroleum jelly to seal the moisture in.

Another Moisturizer... Apply glycerin and rosewater to a slightly moist face.

Eye Openers

Relieving Puffy Eyes... Place a slice of chilled cucumber on each eyelid to relieve tired eyes. Take a 15 minute rest, and enjoy the soothing feeling.

○ Cold tea bags will also relieve tired eyes.

Eye Cream... Castor oil is a terrific moisturizer for the fine area around the eye.

When Blemishes Occur... Dab a drop of lemon juice on blemish to aid the drying process.

○ Or, prepare a solution of 1 cup hot water plus ¼ tsp. salt. Moisten a cotton ball and dab on blemish. Allow to dry and repeat several times. The heat will open the infected pore and the salt will draw the infection.

Makeup Remover... Baby oil is a natural for removing makeup. Freshen up afterwards by dabbing witch hazel on your skin.

Hair-Do's (And Some Don'ts)

Carefree Hair... If you have to brush your hair more than three times during the day to get it in place, it's time for a change of style. Invest in a good haircut and styling. Whether it's a perm or a sleek blunt cut, you'll save valuable time fussing and fiddling.

Give Your Hair A Home Protein Treatment... Use the 'professional's' recipe at home and save costly salon charges. Blend 1 tblsp. lemon juice and 3 whole whipped eggs in the blender. Apply to clean damp hair and allow to set for 15 minutes. Rinse with cool water. This treatment aids damaged ends and leaves hair shining.

Dandruff Shampoo... Simple is the word for this one! Just crush an aspirin tablet until powdered, and add to your normal shampoo. Shake well until powder is dissolved. The acetylsalicylic acid in aspirin is the same ingredient used in many commercial dandruff remedies.

For Oily Hair... Add 2 tblsp. epsom salts to your shampoo bottle and shake until dissolved. When shampooing, rub mainly into the roots and scalp to treat the most oily area. Use every other time you shampoo.

Doubling Shampoo... Commercial shampoo can be diluted with water to half-strength without altering its ability to clean hair.

- Many commercial shampoo bottles have twist off caps that are a nuisance in the shower. Save plastic shampoo or hand lotion bottles that have a flip top applicator and use them for storing shampoo and creme rinse.

- If your family members all seem to have different hair types requiring different shampoos, try switching to baby shampoo which is equally effective on dry, oily and normal hair types.

Dry Shampoo... Baby powder sprinkled on your hair will act as well as any commercial dry shampoo. Brush vigorously.

For Beautiful Highlights... Add the juice of a lemon to a quart of water and apply to hair when rinsing. This will bring out the highlights in blonde hair and is doubly effective if hair is dried naturally in the sun. Brunettes can add a few tablespoons of cider vinegar to the rinse water for extra shining hair.

Hot Oil Treatment For Hair... Give your scalp a hot oil treatment. Wet hair and towel dry. Apply warm vegetable oil or baby oil to hair roots and massage scalp gently. Cover with a warm towel fresh from the dryer. Wait 15 minutes before shampooing.

- ○ Mayonnaise will also condition hair. Apply in the same manner as oil.

Getting Set ... Fill a spray bottle with flat beer to use as a setting lotion.

Cleaning Hair Brushes & Combs ... Fill a basin with warm water and add 2 tblsp. baking soda. Rub brushes together in this solution. Rinse well and pat dry.

Baths & Showers

Extending Bath Powder ... When your box of bath powder is half empty, fill it up with cornstarch and mix well. You will find the mixture both fragrant and soothing.

Footbath ... Everyone needs a soothing footbath now and then. Epsom salts and warm water is wonderful, but if you don't have any, use two handfuls of regular salt instead.

- ○ Another soothing idea is to have two basins, one with hot and the other with cold water. Dunk feet alternately in each basin, ending with the cold water. Doesn't that feel better?

Sheer Luxury ... Soak in the tub for a few moments before adding bath oil. Your skin will have a chance to soak in some moisture before being smoothed by the oil. Baby oil is an inexpensive and delightful bath oil.

- ○ While taking your shower or bath, apply a facial mask. The steam helps your skin absorb the ingredients in the mask and you'll leave the tub with a glowing complexion.

Bath Sachets ... Make your own fragrant bath sachets to keep in linen closets or lingerie drawers. Or, attach a piece of ribbon to the square and hang it in the bath.
You'll need:
2 cups ground, dry pieces of leftover bar soap
4 cups fine rolled oats
1 cup powdered borax
2 tablespoons sachet powder

Mix all ingredients together and spoon into small pastel colored flannelette squares. Gather up edges and tie with ribbon.

When You've Run Out Of Toothpaste ... Use baking soda. It's every bit as effective.

Stain Remover For Teeth ... Brush with lemon juice occasionally to remove tea and coffee stains.

Homemade Mouthwash ... Make your own inexpensive mouthwash. Add a few drops of essence of peppermint (available at drug stores for about one dollar) to a pint of cool water. It leaves your breath smelling sweet and fresh, and costs a mere fraction of its commercial counterpart.

Your Dressing Table

Filing Nails ... Always file nails when perfectly dry from sides to tip. Never back and forth as it will split and roughen edges.

Nail Polish ... Keep nail polish in a cool place, preferably the refrigerator to prevent it from thickening.

- Add a few drops of nail polish remover to thickened nail polish and shake. Results in a smoother finish.

Quick Drying Nail Polish ... Plunge freshly polished nails into ice cold water, but be careful when drying your hands.

Hard As Nails Nail Polish ... Brush baby oil on just polished nails to prevent nicks and chipping.

Perfume ... Keep already opened bottles of perfume in plastic containers in the refrigerator to prevent them from turning rancid.

- Apply a little petroleum jelly wherever you dab on perfume. The scent will last longer.

Lipsticks ... Lipsticks can be used right to the very bottom. Try creating your own color by saving old tubes until you have a few. Using a toothpick scrape the remains into a small butter melter and melt over a low heat. Pour into one of the tubes and refrigerate. You might be surprised at the new color, intended just for you!

Stop Those Rolling Tubes ... Tack a length of elastic to the inside of your cosmetic drawer to keep small tubes from sliding and tipping over.

Tips For The Aching Office Worker

Take The Pressure Off ... Sitting all day at a desk can lead to backaches. Here's a few tips to avoid the problem:

- Don't sit with legs stretched out in front of you. Too much pressure is placed on the lower spine.

- Don't cross your legs. Again this places strain on the lower back.

- Change positions every so often, and take a moment to relieve neck strain by rotating your head in a circular direction. 10 seconds one way, 10 seconds the other way.

- Least of all, make sure the chair you spend 8 hours a day in has good lower back support.

- Don't carry a heavy briefcase (or heavy purse) around with you especially if you carry it in the same hand all the time. Believe it or not, this alone can sway your spine up to 15%. So clean out that purse or attache case.

- Do get some exercise at lunchtime, or take several short walks during the day.

- Even a few deep breaths and some concentrated relaxation will reduce muscle tension.

When The Alarm Clock Fails... The worst way to start the day is by rushing because you're late so keep an entire outfit, everything from stockings to blazer, pressed and ready on hand for late mornings. You'll thank yourself.

Hints For Your Wardrobe

Nylons That Run... The old favorite, clear nail polish, is still the handiest way to stop a run from running.

- Or, try rubbing a bar of soap over the torn stocking.

Emergency Hemming... Use cellophane tape to solve the problem of a hem dropping in midday.

Stretching The Life Of Pantyhose... When one leg has a run, but the other is still good, cut away the unwanted 'leg' at the very top and save the rest. When another pair has a run in it do the same. Soon you will have two matching 'legs', but make sure they are the same brand and shade. Remember too that discarded nylons are great fillers for stuffed pillows and toys.

Felt Hats... Cleaning felt hats is simple if you follow these easy steps: hold the hat over a steaming kettle and brush with a soft brush in the direction of the nap.

Berets... After washing your favorite beret, place a dinner plate inside of it so it will dry to the right size.

Wet Coats... Never hang a wet coat near heat. Hang on a wooden coat hanger in the centre of a well-ventilated room. Brush with a soft brush when dry.

Cleaning Coats With A Nap ... If you own winter coats with a fabric nap, use the 'fabric' attachment to your vacuum cleaner and gently clean the coat by running the vacuum in the direction of the nap.

Repairing Raincoats ... Rubber raincoats that have torn are easily repaired by applying adhesive tape to the inside of the garment along the tear line.

Fur Coats ... Friction will age your expensive fur coat more quickly than any other common cause. Try to avoid repeated friction whenever possible and don't let it rub against other objects in the closet.

What You Should Know About Shoes ... Shoes that are allowed to 'air' for a day between wearings will last a lot longer. Accumulated perspiration tends to destroy linings, so keep this in mind if you tend to overwear your favorite pair.

Canvas Shoes ... Use fabric protector on new canvas shoes to keep them in great shape.

- Clean rope espadrilles by brushing with a small, stiff brush that has been dipped in rug shampoo.

Patent Leathers ... Did you know that petroleum jelly helps prevent cracking and splitting of patent leathers? Try it.

Slippery Shoes ... Avoid slipping on newly purchased shoes by sanding the soles slightly or scraping two or three times on pavement.

Heels That Have Worn ... Have worn heels replaced as soon as possible to prevent destroying the shape of the shoe.

Repairing Scuffs On Your Favorite Kid Leather Shoes ... Gently lift the torn leather and place a small dot of rubber cement on its underside. Wait a moment and press back into place. Allow to dry and rub away any excess glue with your fingers.

Shoe Polish ... If you've run out of shoe polish, try using paste floor wax. It's a great substitute and its neutral color works well on light or dark leather.

- Furniture polish will shine leather shoes in a jiffy.

- Use nail polish remover to rid white shoes of tar or grease.

Squeaks ... Silence those squeaking shoes by piercing the sole with a darning needle four or five times at the ball of the foot.

When Boots Go Into Hibernation... Keep winter boots longer by taking a few minutes of preparation at the end of the winter season. Clean boots thoroughly with leather cleaner and allow to dry. (It's a good time to apply water repellent for next year's use). Stuff the insides with old newspaper, or if available, stiff cardboard. Store standing up.

Wet Boots?... Nothing can feel quite so chilling as having to step into damp winter boots. If time permits, use your hair dryer by placing the nozzle in the top of each boot. Set at high and hold in position for five minutes. Makes sure all zippers or laces are undone for better air circulation. This tip is guaranteed to warm the soles!

Jewelery

Broken Bead Necklaces... Use dental floss to restring bead or pearl necklaces.

A Jewel Of An Idea... Keep fine gold and silver chains from knotting in your jewelery box by cutting a plastic straw to measure half the length of the chain less ¼". Slip the chain through the straw and fasten the catch.

Sparkling Diamonds... Dip your diamonds in a pot boiling water to which several drops of ammonia and a spoonful of Ivory soapflakes have been added. Use a tea strainer. Hold for a few seconds, then remove and rinse in cold water. Soak for 5 minutes in alcohol, and finally rinse and pat dry.

Costume Jewelery... Rubbing alcohol will clean costume jewellery if allowed to soak for several minutes. Wipe dry with a soft cloth.

Old-Fashioned Jewelery Cleaner... A tried and true formula!

    1 oz. dry borax
    ½ oz. washing soda
    ½ oz. castile soap shavings
    2 ½ oz. liquid ammonia
    1 pint water

Mix first three ingredients in a pint of water and boil until dissolved. Partly cool, and stir in liquid ammonia. Add enough water to make two quarts. When ready to use, place jewelery in enamel pan, cover with solution and bring to a boil. Using a soft brush (toothbrush or mascara brush) rub jewelery gently and rinse in hot water. Pat dry.

The Last Word

The Best Hint Of All ... Now that your house is in great shape, what about you? Run, jog, skip, dance, swim, ski — whatever you like to do, do it! You'll get double the amount of energy back, and be a lot more radiant for it.

NOTES:

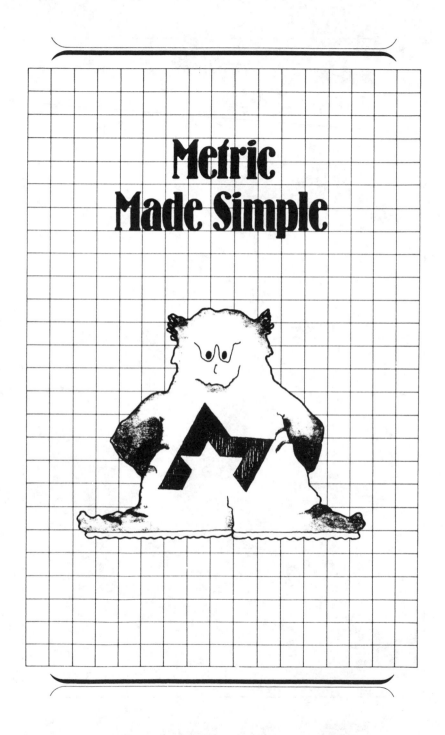

NOTES:

THE METRIC SYSTEM

Metric Mathematics... If you can multiply and divide by 10, you think in metric. Changing from one multiple or submultiple of a unit to another is done by simply moving the decimal point (e.g. 100 cm = 1 m.).

Thinking Metric... If you can associate specific metric measurements with a visual experience or activity (e.g. a metre is the length of a long step, normal room temperature is 21°C) ... it's easy! And there are only 7 base units compared to 53 in the imperial system.

Area (Square Measure):

1 square centimetre	=	100 sq. millimetres	=	0.15 sq. inches
1 square metre	=	100 sq. centimetres	=	10.8 sq. feet
1 square dekametre	=	100 sq. metres		
1 square hectometre (hectare)	=	10,000 sq. metres	=	2.5 acres
10 hectares	=	1 sq. kilometre		

Knowing:	Multiply by:	To obtain:
square inches	6.5	square centimetres
square feet	0.09	square metres
square yards	0.8	square metres
square miles	2.6	square kilometres
acres	0.4	hectares
square centimetres	0.16	square inches
square metres	1.2	square yards
square kilometres	0.4	square miles
hectares (10,000m²)	2.5	acres

Lengths

1 centimetre **(cm)**	=	10 millimetres **(mm)**	=	0.3937 inches
1 decimetre **(dm)**	=	10 centimetres		
1 metre **(m)**	=	10 decimetres		
1 dekametre **(dk)**	=	10 metres		
1 hectometre **(hm)**	=	10 dekametres		
1 kilometre **(km)**	=	10 hectometres		

Quick Conversions ... If you know a length and need to convert to either metric or standard, simply multiply by the number given.

Knowing:	Multiply by:	To obtain:
millimetres	0.04	inches
centimetres	0.4	inches
metres	3.3	feet
metres	1.1	yards
kilometres	0.6	miles
inches	2.5	centimetres
feet	30	centimetres
yards	0.9	metres
miles	1.6	kilometres

Even Quicker ... We're giving you charts for at a glance conversions.

Inches	=	Centimetres
1 in	=	2.5 cm
6 ins	=	15 cm
8 ins	=	20 cm
10 ins	=	25 cm
12 ins (1 ft)	=	30 cm
14 ins	=	35 cm
36 ins (1 yd)	=	90 cm
40 ins	=	100 cm (1 metre)
4 ft	=	1.2 m
5 ft	=	1.5 m
6 ft	=	1.8 m
7 ft	=	2.0 m

Travelling Lengths:

Mileage to Kilometres ... When converting miles to kilometres, take the number of 10's in the mileage figure and multiply by 6. Add this number to the number of miles to arrive at total kilometres. Example: 90 miles (9 x 6 = 54 + 90 = 144 km).

Kilometres to Miles ... Divide this number of kilometres by 3 and multiply by 2. Example: 96 km divided by 3 = 32 x 2 = 64 miles.

Miles	=	**Kilometres**
1 mile	=	1.6 km
5	=	8
10	=	16
30	=	48
50	=	80
75	=	120
100	=	161

Determining Gas Consumption ... Have your gas tank filled and make a notation of the odometre reading. On the next fill up, divide the number of litres of gasoline it took to fill the car into the number of kilometres travelled since the last fill up to arrive at the number of kilometres travelled per litre of gas consumption.

If you are still thinking in terms of miles per gallon, use this handy reference to measure the efficiency of your car:

10.65 km per litre is equivalent to 30 miles per gallon
8.88 km per litre is equivalent to 25 miles per gallon
7.11 km per litre is equivalent to 20 miles per gallon
5.33 km per litre is equivalent to 15 miles per gallon
3.55 km per litre is equivalent to 10 miles per gallon

Temperature

Knowing:	Multiply by:	To obtain:
Degrees centigrade	1.8 (then add 32)	Farenheit temperature
Degrees farenheit	5/9 (after subtracting 32)	Celsius temperature

0°C (32°F)... is the freezing point of water
10°C (50°F)... is the temperature of a warm winter day
20°C (68°F)... is the temperature of a mild spring day and the new recommended central heating living room temperature (cooler than you've been used to)
30°C (86°F)... is the temperature of a hot summer's day
37°C (98°F)... is normal body temperature
40°C (104°F)... is heatwave hot
43°C (110°F)... is hot bath temperature
49°C (119°F)... is hand-hot water temperature
100°C (212°F)... is the boiling point of water

Oven Temperatures ... for the range of temperatures used for cooking, the number of degrees Farenheit is about twice the number of degrees Celsius.

Meat Probe:

Meat	Degree of Doneness	Internal Temperature
Beef	Rare	60ºC
	Medium	65ºC
	Well done	75ºC
Veal	Well done	80ºC
Lamb	Rare	60ºC
	Medium	70ºC
	Well done	75ºC
Pork	Fresh	80ºC
Ham	Cured	55ºC
	Ready to serve	70ºC
Poultry		85ºC

Fresh Fish: For each 3 cm thickness bake 10 min at 230ºC.

Frozen Fish: For each 3 cm thickness bake 20 min at 230ºC.

Tip: When baking in ovenproof glassware, reduce oven temperature by 10ºC.

Volume

1 centilitre	=	10 millilitres
1 decilitre	=	10 centilitres
1 litre	=	10 decilitres
1 decalitre	=	10 litres
1 hectolitre	=	10 decalitres
1 kilolitre	=	10 hectolitres

Common Conversions ... When converting your recipes to metric, round either upward or downward but be consistent with all measurements.

5 millilitres **(ml)**	=	1 teaspoon
10 millilitres **(ml)**	=	1 tablespoon
50 millilitres **(ml)**	=	¼ cup (60 ml, to be exact)
100 millilitres **(ml)**	=	½ cup (120 ml, to be exact)
200 millilitres **(ml)**	=	¾ cup (180 ml, to be exact)
250 millilitres **(ml)**	=	1 cup (240 ml, to be exact)

Knowing:	Multiply by:	To obtain:
teaspoons	5	millilitres
tablespoons	15	millilitres
fluid ounces	30	millilitres
cups	0.24	litres
pints	0.56	litres
quarts	1.1	litres
gallons	4.5	litres
cubic feet	0.03	cubic metres
cubic yards	0.76	cubic metres
millilitres	0.03	fluid ounces
litres	1.75	pints
litres	0.87	quarts
litres	0.22	gallons
cubic metres	35	cubic feet
cubic metres	1.3	cubic yards

Weights

1 centigram	=	10 milligrams
1 decigram	=	10 centigrams
1 gram	=	10 decigrams
1 decagram	=	10 grams
1 hectogram	=	10 decagrams
1 kilogram	=	10 hectograms
1,000 grams	=	2.2 pounds
25 grams (g)	=	just under 1 oz
100 grams	=	3.6 oz
400 grams	=	just under 1 lb

Pounds to Kilograms ... Divide by 2 and subtract 10%.
Example: 140 lbs. divided by 2 = 70 - 10% or 7 = 63 kg.

Knowing:	Multiply by:	To obtain:
ounces	28	gram
pounds	0.45	kilograms
short tons (2000 lb)	0.9	tons

Kilograms to Pounds ... Multiply by 2 and add 10%.
Example: 110 kg x 2 = 240 + 10% or 11 = 251 lbs.

Knowing:	Multiply by:	To obtain:
grams	0.035	ounces
kilograms	2.2	pounds
tonnes (100 kg)	1.1	short tons

SHOPPERS GUIDE

Food	Supermarket Unit	Yield
Meats:		
Boneless: ground meat	500 g	4 servings
Medium Bone: roasts, chops, steaks	800 g	4 servings
Boney Cuts: spareribs	1.5 kg	4-5 servings
Bacon, sliced	500 g	22-24 slices
Poultry:		
Chicken breasts and legs	1 kg	4 servings
Chicken wings	1 kg	3 servings
Turkey	4 kg	8-10 servings
Fish & Seafood		
Fillets	500 g	3-4 servings
Steaks	500 g	3 servings
Scallops, shrimps & lobster	500 g	4 servings
Dairy Products:		
Milk	1 L	5 glasses (200 mL each)
Milk powder	100 g	1 L fluid milk
Cottage Cheese	500 g	4 servings (125 mL each)
Butter or Margarine	500 g	530 mL
Produce:		
Apples, Peaches, Pears	500 g	3-4 medium
Bananas	500 g	4 small
Onions	500 g	4-5 medium
Potatoes	500 g	4 medium
Tomatoes	500 g	3-4 medium

EMERGENCY SUBSTITUTES

For	Substitute
250 ml cake & pastry flour	220 ml all-purpose flour
15 ml cornstarch	30 ml flour
5 ml baking powder	2 ml baking soda plus 3 ml cream of tartar
250 ml milk	125 ml evaporated milk plus 125 ml water
250 ml skim milk	45 ml skim milk powder plus 250 ml water
250 ml sour milk or buttermilk	15 ml lemon juice or vinegar plus milk
250 ml table cream (18%)	225 ml milk plus 45 ml butter
1 whole egg	2 egg yolks
1 square unsweetened chocolate	50 ml cocoa plus 15 ml fat
250 ml honey	175 ml sugar plus 50 ml liquid
1 clove garlic	0.5 ml garlic powder
1 small onion	15 ml onion flakes

NOTES:

NOTES:

Index

Ache, to relieve back, 107; to relieve tooth, 88
Ailments, to treat minor, 88
Alternator, car, 62
Animals, see Pets
Antiques, to clean, 29; refinishing, 48, 49
Ants, to eliminate, 37
Apples, baked, 7; non-browning, 12; pie (see Pies)
Appliances, to clean, 19; mechanical problems, 55, 56, 57
Art, preserving children's, 85
Astringent, facial, 104

Baby, when bathing, 85; toys, 85; night feedings, 85
Bacon, prevent curling, 16; drippings, 16; leftovers, 17
Baking Powder, substitution, 7
Baking Soda, as deodorizer, 20; as cleaner, 21
Banana, too ripe, 12
Bath, powder, 106; sachets, 106; to relax, 106
Bathtub, to remove stains, 34; to remove decals, 34
Bathroom, to clean, 33-34
Battery, car, 61
Beads, to restring, 110
Beauty, tips, 103, 104, 105, 106, 107
Beverage, to chill, 23
Blemishes, to treat, 104
Blender, to clean, 19; mechanical problem, 55
Boards, wooden bread-to clean, 22
Books, storing & protecting, 37
Boots, to dry, 110; to store, 110
Bottles, hard to open, 23; baby-to clean, 85; baby-keeping warm, 85
Brakes, car, 58
Bread, heating, 9; toast, 9; uses for stale, 9; making crumbs, 10
Broadloom, see Carpets
Brown Sugar, see Sugar
Brushes, hair-to clean, 106
Brussels Sprouts, to eliminate odor, 12
Bugs, to eliminate, 37, 38
Burrs, to remove, 39
Butter, measuring when hard, 9; extending, 10
Button Holes, when sewing, 79
Buttons, when sewing, 79

Cabbage, eliminate cooking odor, 12
Cables, electrical, 50
Cake, cutting or slicing, 7; keeping moist, 7, 8; non-stick, 7; when freezing, 18; decorating utensil substitution, 8

Can Opener, cleaning, 19; mechanical problem, 56
Candles, 36
Cane, furniture-to tighten, 29
Canvas, shoes-to clean, 109
Car Maintenance, 57
Cards, playing, 37
Carpentry, 48
Carpet, to clean, 29, 30, 31; stain remover, 31; burns, 31; eliminate sliding, 31; beaters, 31; raising pile, 30; rejuvenate, 30; homemade shampoo, 30; fraying, 30; car-removing salt, 61; removing glue, 30
Cast Iron, cookware-to clean, 21
Cauliflower, eliminate cooking odor, 12; maintain whiteness, 14
Celery, use for tops, 13
Chains, jewelery-to store, 110
Chamois, to soften, 72
Chapped Skin, to treat, 88
Cheese, when dried, 10; adding to pastry, 7
Cheesecloth, treatment, 27
Chicken, see Poultry
Children, tips & ideas, 85, 86, 87, 88
China, to clean, 21; cracked, 21; storage, 21
Chocolate, substitute for, 7; mint icing, 8
Chrome, to clean, 35
Cinnamon, as cake topping, 8; as room deodorizer, 20
Clams, to open, 15
Cleaning, appliances, 19, 20; artificial plants, 35; bathroom, 33; blender, 19; breadboards, 22; can openers, 19; carpets, 29, 30, 31; china, 21; copper, 21; cookware, 21, crystal, 21, 36; fireplaces, 36; floors, 31; frames, 35; furniture, 27, 28, 29; general household, 27; glassware, 21; garage, 54; kettles, 22; lampshades, 36; marble, 36; pans/pots, 20; pewter, 35; piano keys, 35; plastic utensils, 20; place mats (straw), 22; porcelain, 36; sinks, 22; silver, 35; vases, 35; walls, 31; windows, 33; woodwork, 31
Closets, to avoid dampness, 37
Clothes, washing, 67; your wardrobe, 108
Coats, winter-when wet, 108; winter-fur, 109; winter-with nap, 109; rain-to repair, 109
Cockroaches, to eliminate, 37
Cocoa, as chocolate substitute, 7
Coconut, toasting, 8
Coffee, economizing, 16; freezing, 16; iced, 16; maintaining freshness, 16; Maker, mechanical problems, 55
Cookie Cutter, to prevent sticking, 7
Copper, to clean, 21
Corkscrew, to substitute for, 22